ALEUTS

Survivors of the Bering Land Bridge

by

WILLIAM S. LAUGHLIN

University of Connecticut

HOLT, RINEHART AND WINSTON

New York   Chicago   San Francisco   Dallas
Montreal   Toronto   London   Sydney

To
Leslie Finney Laughlin
Afenogin K. Ermeloff
Eva Chercasen
Ales Hrdlicka

Figs. 4, 18, 20, 22, 24, 25, 29, and Table 6.1 from Science, *1975, Vol. 189. Copyright 1975 by the American Association for the Advancement of Science.*
Fig. 7 courtesy of the National Anthropological Archives.
Fig. 23 courtesy of Mary McDowell.
Fig. 28 courtesy of Anita Stocklin.
Fig. 31 reproduced from "The First Americans: Origins, Affinities, and Adaptations" with permission; published by Gustav Fischer, New York-Stuttgart, © The Wenner-Gren Foundation for Anthropological Research, Inc.
Fig. 32 from D. M. Hopkins (ed.), The Bering Land Bridge. *Copyright 1967 by Stanford University Press.*
Fig. 34 from Arctic Anthropology, 1966, Vol. III, No. 2. Copyright 1966 by the Regents of the University of Wisconsin.
Fig. 40 courtesy of Susan B. Beman.

Library of Congress Cataloging in Publication Data

Laughlin, William S
    Aleuts: survivors of the Bering Land Bridge.

    (Case studies in cultural anthropology)
    Bibliography: p. 148
    1. Aleuts. I. Title. II. Series.
E99.A34L38   970.004'97   80–12594
ISBN 0–03–081269–0

Foreword

About the Series

These case studies in cultural anthropology are designed to bring to students, in beginning and intermediate courses in the social sciences, insights into the richness and complexity of human life as it is lived in different ways and in different places. They are written by men and women who have lived in the societies they write about and who are professionally trained as observers and interpreters of human behavior. The authors are also teachers, and in writing their books they have kept the students who will read them foremost in their minds. It is our belief that when an understanding of ways of life very different from one's own is gained, abstractions and generalizations about social structure, cultural values, subsistence techniques, and the other universal categories of human social behavior become meaningful.

About the Author

William S. Laughlin was born in Canton, Missouri, and raised in Salem, Oregon, where he attended Willamette University. He first visited the Aleutian and Commander Islands in 1938 as a student member of a Smithsonian Field Expedition under the direction of Dr. Aleš Hrdlička. He subsequently studied at Haverford College and Bryn Mawr College before receiving his Ph.D. degree from Harvard University in 1949. He has done fieldwork in Siberia, Alaska, Canada, and Greenland, as well as in the continental United States. Many of the field studies made by Dr. Laughlin were multidisciplinary and included students and scholars from other nations. He taught at the University of Oregon and the University of Wisconsin before moving to the University of Connecticut, where he is Chairman of the Laboratory of Biological Anthropology and Professor of Biobehavioral Sciences. He has been a Fulbright Fellow in Denmark, a Fellow at the Center for Advanced Study in the Behavioral Sciences, and was awarded a piece of land on which to build a home by the Native Village of Nikolski in 1971. In addition to his researches, he has represented the Aleuts in state and federal courts.

About the Book

In this case study, Dr. Laughlin has provided us with a rare integration of ethnological, demographic, biological, archeological, and ecological data and interpretations about a single people with a recognizable history of 9000 years. Anthropology, the study of human life in its totality, has, since its beginnings in the late nineteenth century, claimed to be the one social science that encompassed all of these dimensions of human life and the conditions of its existence. Alfred Kroeber once described anthropology as a kind of holding company subsuming all of the other disciplines concerned with the (then) study of man.

With increasing technical knowledge and professionalization these academically separable branches of the "mother" discipline have tended to go their separate ways to the extent that they have become distinctive subdisciplines. Only in the introductory course do most anthropologists give even lip service to the interdependency of these various dimensions of life. The emergence of biocultural anthropology and of sociobiology has challenged this separation, and many practitioners of the highly specialized subdisciplines of anthropology are looking for what some call "materialist" factors, including the biological as well as economic and ecological processes of human adaptation. The relevance and interdependency of all factors—genetic, demographic, ecological, symbolic, and structural—is being recognized as the search goes on for a more comprehensive understanding of the human condition.

Dr. Laughlin's case study of the Aleuts is in the forefront of this trend and takes the integration of factors and processes that are ordinarily left separated further than most studies. It is unique in this series and virtually unmatched elsewhere.

This case study is more than an interdisciplinary *tour de force*. It is about a most interesting people, the Aleuts, whose long history has much to teach us about living in this world. Their knowledge, their longevity, and their survival power are worthy of serious study. We are fortunate that they have been studied in such a way as to make it possible to grasp something of their material as well as their symbolic adaptations.

GEORGE AND LOUISE SPINDLER
General Editors

Calistoga, California

Acknowledgments

My first experience with the Aleuts was so stimulating that I returned in 1948 and many more times after that, and made many Aleut friends in several villages. Though not an Aleut, Gordon H. Marsh, now Father Innocent, provided an indispensable introduction to linguistics and the Aleut language in the field. He compiled formidable ethnographic records and excavated as well. Mrs. Mae Ermeloff did much of the early translation, and Mrs. Agnes Sovoroff provided valuable commentary and additions. Mr. Afenogin K. Ermeloff and Mrs. Eva Chercasen were enduring friends for many years. They typified the intellectual knowledge, technical skills, helpfulness, and concern for truth that are the hallmarks of Aleut culture and found in every Aleut village.

I have drawn heavily on the cooperation of Albert B. Harper, who participated in the excavations of the ill-fated Denis Medvedev party and on Anangula in 1970, conducted the anthropometry of Aleuts in 1973, and worked with the Soviet team in the Aleutians in 1974 and in Siberia in 1975. His construction of life tables has been valuable to both the Aleuts and to this book. Sara B. Laughlin worked five seasons and, with Mary McDowell, is responsible for many facts and insights into the stratigraphy of Anangula and Chaluka. Bruno Frohlich and Jorgen B. Jorgensen of Denmark, and Joëlle Robert-Lamblin of France brought additional international comparisons. I have drawn on Susan Beman's study of skeletal biology of the Kagamil mummy population, as well as her field research in the Aleutians. Her editorial skills have been especially valuable. Ruth F. Laughlin worked in the Aleutians with Aleuts and with the Soviet team of A.P. Okladnikov, and has entertained Aleuts in our home. Beverly Holmes' years of experience on Unalaska and her knowledge of Russian have been helpful. Christy G. Turner, in addition to his archeological and his later dental studies, was the first to call attention to the fact that Umnak Island had been the terminus of the Bering Land Bridge.

I am grateful for "the small piece of land on which to build a home," given me in 1971 by the Native Village of Nikolski. It is happily located on Chaluka, with a view of Anangula. I can also see the Monument House, a small structure enclosing the stump of a very tall pole that stood there before the arrival of the Russians, and enjoy knowing that as long as that ancient remnant endures the Aleut people will endure.

Contents

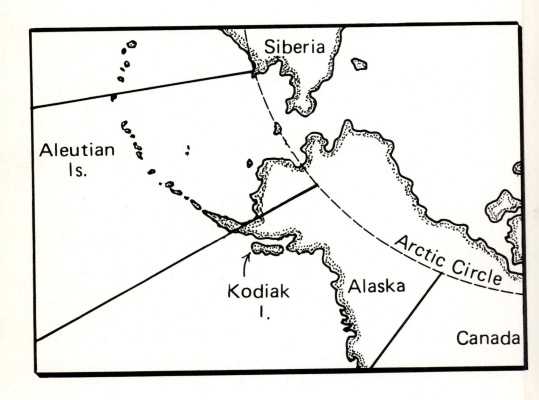

1 / Introduction

ORGANIZATIONAL STRATEGY

The organizational strategy of this book places the Aleut people first, and then relates them to their natural environment, to the things they have done—their hunting and intellectual achievements, and to the length of time they have been in the Aleutians. Physically, linguistically, culturally, and geographically, the Aleuts are a highly distinctive people. The dimensions and structure of their distinctiveness are presented in separate chapters, each with a focus on an area important to Aleut life and history. The degree of their distinctiveness is best evaluated by comparison with other peoples. However, the major emphasis of this book is directly on the Aleuts and comparisons are, therefore, limited to those that help us secure a true picture of these people.

For each major feature or characteristic—whether of the people, the culture, or the environment—there is variation and there are changes over time. Three concepts—major feature, variation, and change—provide a working paradigm for organization.

The interrelations between major features are equally interesting and are perhaps among the most attractive features of the Aleuts and their environment. An unusually high number of connections or correspondences exist between the people and their culture, language and environment, each of which illuminates others and helps to explain the overall strategy of Aleut adaptation to their circumstances.

INFORMATION MATRIX

The entire corpus of the Aleut people, culture, and environment may be viewed as an information matrix. Among the key items in the Aleut information matrix are the presence of:

1. *One population system,* originally of Aleuts only inside their domain, and characterized by noteworthy longevity.
2. *One language,* understood only by Aleuts, with three major geographic dialects, a rich oral culture, elaboration in various areas of cultural interest, and unusual capability in counting into high numbers.
3. *Stable and productive marine environment,* with considerable abundance and diversity.
4. *Directional configuration of the geographic domain,* a longitudinal and linear

1

distribution of islands that directed gene flow and the diffusion of cultural traits along an east–west axis and promoted a relatively high degree of isolation.

5. *Rich material culture* in which each Aleut owned many possessions, of which a large proportion contained durable materials (stone, bone and ivory) with remarkable elaboration in kayaks (*baidarkas*) and umiaks (*baidars*), clothing, and mummies.

6. *Complex intellectual culture*, including a sophisticated knowledge of human anatomy, and with contact, their own written language in their special alphabet.

7. *Village midden sites* with quantities of Aleut skeletons and Russian Cossack skeletons in later times, artifacts, and faunal remains. These sites include many fire hearths suitable for radiocarbon dating, and their elevation is related to the sea level appropriate to the time they were occupied.

8. *Cultural continuities over time.* An appreciable amount of information is shared or transferred from living Aleuts to the registration of Russian artifacts, to the mummy caves, to the most recent archeological levels, to the earlier levels of the same sites, to the Transition culture and back to the initial Asiatic template of the Anangula site.

9. *Correspondences* exist in rich profusion between dialect and breeding isolates, material traits and religious beliefs (image of the deity and mummies), economy and social organization, tools and animals, reefs and villages. When each trait is examined for its form, function, use, and meaning, many connections between the form of an object and its use are automatically revealed in the Aleut name of the thing, or in its parts.

10. *Living Aleuts.* Some of the Aleuts still occupy old sites and they provide information based upon experience as well as on memory. Their survival has permitted the simultaneous study of physical anthropology, language, ethnology, and archeology.

11. *Bering Land Bridge origin.* The great age of the Anangula blade, burin, and core site situated at the terminus of the older Bering Land Bridge, together with the much more recent ages of the sites at the western and eastern extremities of the Aleut domain which lack this Asiatic unifacial tool complex, indicate the first inhabitants came in from an older coastline of the former Bering Land Bridge and subsequently expanded in two directions from there to the east and to the west. The sharp linguistic boundary between Aleut and Eskimo is the result of the eastward migration of Aleuts from their earliest occupation on Umnak Island.

The exacting experiential and performance world in which the Aleuts lived, their pragmatic and inventive attitude toward the world, and their high regard for skill and knowledge are all part of their adaptive achievement as individuals and as a population. Both the people and their situation are informative.

The strategy of chapter organization rests upon the desire to present the activities and achievements of the Aleuts and to trace their interrelationships. Spotlighting this small Aleut primer is a concern to demonstrate how information has been derived for examining, testing, and then arriving at the conclusions that form the overall picture of Aleut behavior.

There is a "need to know" that is common to students, Aleuts, scientists, and judges. Beginning with cogently argued petitions to the Russian government in the nineteenth century and continuing with current court cases with the United States government, Aleut affairs are increasingly affected by agency decisions and by formal court decisions. I have been impressed with the need to know and to control a considerable span of information in order to focus on one point and to demonstrate its validity. The favorable decisions that have been handed down reflect in part the ability to answer specifically with facts those questions which are asked. Adversary proceedings do have the merit of encouraging the preparation of a solid factual basis for a conclusion. Therefore, this is not a book of revelations nor is it designed for entertainment. Whether a college freshman, an Aleut teenager, a research scientist, or a judge, the student should find this book an orderly, coherent abstract and a useful outline or map to understanding the origins, rise and fall, and frequent recovery of the Aleuts from the perilous challenges of nature and time that have been their companions for 9000 years.

2/The Aleut people: Unangan

INTRODUCTION

"Who is an Aleut" turns out to be a definition of scientific, historical, and legal interest. The Aleutian Aleuts designated themselves by the term *unangan*, "people." The term *Aleut* is of uncertain origin and was applied to them by the Russians. At first, the word was used only for the inhabitants of the Near Islands, and only later to all Aleut speakers. Unfortunately, it was also later applied to the Koniag Eskimos as well as to other southern Eskimos. These were the populations who came to be designated as civilized, settled, or dependent. Various censuses, including those of the United States, regularly flounder on the categorization of Aleuts and Koniag Eskimos. The Koniag Eskimos may call themselves Aleuts even though they speak Eskimo. The ambiguity in designation is important to the populations involved, to their legal representation, land claims, citizenship status at various times in the past, and to their enrollment on various rosters, such as those related to the Alaska Land Settlement Act.

The essential fact is that Aleuts and Koniag Eskimos cannot speak to each other; their languages are mutually unintelligible. Early books published by Veniaminov and Netzvietov in the 1830s and 1840s specified Aleutian-Fox or Atka dialects, in contrast to Tischnov's Aleutian-Kodiak alphabet of 1848. The term *Aleut* is synonymous with the Aleut population. The Aleuts extended without interruption from Attu Island in the west to the Shumagin Islands on the south side of the Alaska Peninsula and to Port Moller on the north side. Hrdlička remarked: ". . . that on no occasion did the Aleuts include the Koniags among their relations, but were constantly fighting with them" (Hrdlička, 1945, p. 31).

PHYSICAL CHARACTERISTICS

The Aleuts are typically Mongoloid in appearance. They have large heads, straight black hair, dark brown eyes, Mongoloid eyefolds, medium to small noses, and very broad faces with prominent cheekbones. They are short in stature with long trunks and short legs. Hands and feet are small, broad, and muscular. The men are powerfully built with high muscle relief and very little fat, even in old age. Both men and women are lightly pigmented with a tendency toward rosy cheeks. Women especially have fine complexions (see Fig. 1).

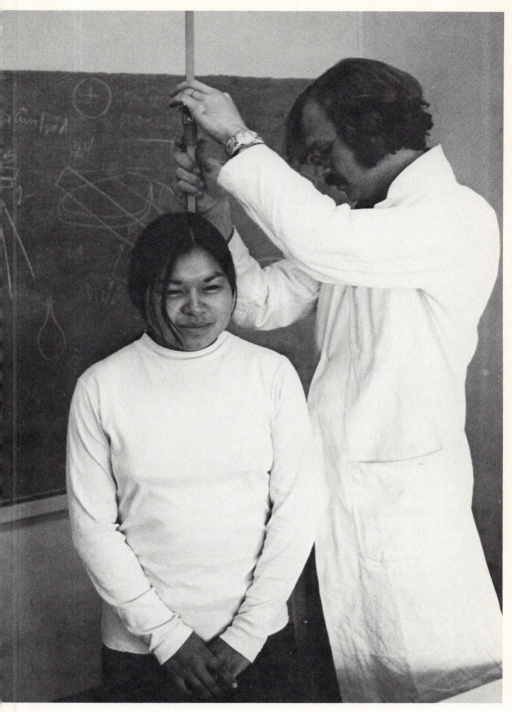

Fig. 1. Measuring stature with an anthropometer, 1973. Miss Clara Dushkin of Nikolski and A. B. Harper.

The face, neck, and hands are characteristically tanned by exposure, whereas the remainder of the body remains only lightly pigmented. Babies sometimes display a sacral spot at birth, a normal patch of bluish color at the base of the spinal column, which disappears within one year. The old Aleut explanation of this pigmentation is that the baby was reluctant to be born and had to be kicked out by a spirit.

The skeletons confirm the muscular appearance, with unusually large prominences on the upper arm bone, as well as large and well-defined muscle attachments generally. The mandibular torus is a characterizing trait of the Aleuts. This is an elevation of bone varying in size but roughly similar to an elongated button, situated in the region of the canine and premolar teeth, on either half of the lingual surface of the mandible. It is visible in the living and even more obvious on the mandibles of the skeletons. The mandibular torus appears in young children and is more frequent in men than in women. These two facts are part of the evidence indicating the predominantly genetic origin of this trait rather than a functional origin resulting from chewing stress. Young children have not had time to chew very much tough food or fabricational materials, and women chew much more tough material than men. If the trait were due to stress, then the women, whose teeth are much more worn than those of men and who actually chew more skins (especially for the preparation of boot soles), should have a higher frequency of mandibular torus than men. There is also a difference between eastern Aleuts (61 percent) and western Aleuts (26 percent). It reduces with the loss of the teeth.

The mandibular torus reflects the more Mongoloid ancestry of the Aleuts, contrasted with American Indians in whom the trait is much less frequent. Another difference between Aleuts and Indians is the higher proportion of palatine tori (a bony elevation along the midline of the palate) to mandibular tori found in Indians. A significant difference has not been found between the earlier Paleo-Aleuts and the later Neo-Aleuts.

The teeth tend to be large with especially large upper lateral incisors in relation to the middle incisors. On their lingual surface (tongue side) they display a depression between marginal ridges that can easily be felt or seen with a mirror. This trait is commonly known as "shoveling." By looking into the mouth, we see several traits of the crowns of the teeth, which, as a group, are known as the "Mongoloid dental complex." This syndrome is found in both deciduous and permanent dentition. Most obvious is the frequent absence of the third molars, or presence of a very small, peg-shaped molar. Three-rooted first lower molars are common, especially in males. This trait can be seen with the aid of an X ray, in the extracted tooth, or in the root sockets. These phenomena are important in establishing the continuity between the living Aleuts and their ancestors who are interred in mummy caves and are buried in village middens. The traits are also important in demonstrating the Mongoloid and Asiatic affinities of the Aleuts.

When the breadth of the head, or cranium, is expressed as a percentage of the length of the head, the resulting cephalic index provides a useful measure of the proportion of breadth to length. This form of index is of considerable use inside population systems rather than for comparisons between unrelated peoples. Interestingly, there are two variations—one in geographic distribution and one in time —that characterize the Aleut population. The eastern Aleuts have relatively broader and, therefore, rounder heads than the western Aleuts (cephalic index of 84 for the eastern region contrasted with 82 for the western). The earlier skeletal population, the Paleo-Aleuts, have much narrower heads (cranial index of 73) than the later Neo-Aleuts (Table 2.1). Currently, the most plausible interpretation of this change over time and the geographical variation is that the most rapid evolution took place in head form in the eastern Aleutians and spread from there to the western Aleutians. This corresponds well to the overall picture derived from three facts—the greater time depth in the east, the greater population size, and the directional configuration of the islands that favored the movements of genes and people from east to west, after the original expansion from the Samalga Pass region, to both east and west.

ALEUT–ESKIMO AFFINITIES AND ORIGINS

The Aleuts are of special significance, both physically and culturally, in studies of the original populating of the New World. It appears that no less than three major migrations have penetrated into America from Siberia. These are most quickly surveyed by examination of the major blood groups:

Aleuts and Eskimos	B	A	O
North American Indians	–	A	O
South American Indians	–	–	O

The Aleuts and the Eskimos are more similar to each other than they are to Indians, and they show the greatest similarity to Asiatic populations. It is not yet possible to state that they are more similar to Asiatic populations than they are to American Indians, but it is certain that they are more similar to Asiatic populations than are American Indians. Both the Aleuts and Eskimos are separated from American Indians by dental traits, variations in the spinal column, the size and form of the mandible, blood groups, and many other characteristics. When viewing the human species as a whole, these are minor differences. Upon closer examination, these differences are very useful in the ethnic identification of the people, in their evolutionary history, and in some cases, in the explanation of their physical health.

TABLE 2.1   SEQUENCE OF CRANIAL AND CEPHALIC INDEX

	Male			*Female*		
	n	*range*	*mean*	*n*	*range*	*mean*
Eastern Aleuts						
(cephalic index of living)	17	81.0–89.0	84.6	17	78.0–91.0	84.3
Kagamil Mummies	11	75.8–85.2	81.4	9	79.4–86.9	83.4
Chaluka: West End	6	74.4–85.1	78.8	4	75.1–87.1	80.9
Chaluka: East End (earliest)	7	69.8–76.4	73.8	8	64.9–74.2	71.3

Cephalic index may be compared with cranial index by subtracting two index units from the cephalic index.

Among Aleuts, there is a high frequency of two vertebral column defects: separate neural arches and *spina bifida*. (The two conditions may occur together.) Both these traits are shared with Eskimos, who have the world's highest frequency of separate neural arches. This is one of the primary traits distinguishing Aleuts and Eskimos from American Indians.

A trait which Aleuts share with Eskimos, and which distinguishes them from Russians and American Indians, is the very large mandible. The difference is seen most clearly in the form of the vertical portion of the mandible, the ascending

Figure 1a.   Nikolski Bay with Mountains, 1974. Nikolski Bay with Mt. Vesvidof (active) and Mt. Rechesnoi (inactive) in the background. Soviet archeologists V.E. Larichev and A. Konopatkski on left, W.S. Laughlin, A.P. Okladnikov, and A.P. Derevyanko on right.

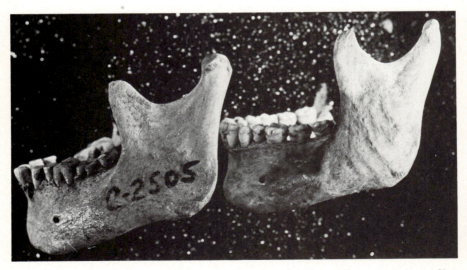

Fig. 2. Mandibles of a Russian of 1764 A.D. and an Aleut. The ramus (ascending portion) of the Aleut is very broad and low. The Russian ramus is narrower and higher. Eskimos are similar to Aleuts in this trait, and differ markedly from Indians, who are more similar to the European-Russian type.

ramus. In both Aleuts and Eskimos, this is very broad and low. Figure 2 shows the contrasting configuration of an Aleut mandible and a Russian mandible.

The large and massive mandible has not changed significantly over a period of 4000 years. However, the vault (the upper portion of the skull) has changed in form from narrow to broad. Within the Aleutian sequence, there is an intermediate form late in time at Chaluka. Only a few examples of this type have been reported, however, such as the Aleut killed with the Medvedev party (see Chapter 10). Broad heads are reported as early as 780 A.D. for Akun Island in the east.

The geographical and historical stability of the mandible and the variability of the skull vault illustrate a fundamental aspect of the entire Aleut–Eskimo stock. The Aleuts developed the broadest heads of all related tribes (Fig. 3). They are well distinguished from the nearest Koniag Eskimos by this characteristic. There is a smaller disparity in head size between the western Yupik Eskimos and the Inupiaq Eskimos, who extend from Alaska to Greenland.

Another characteristic of the head is the low height of the Aleut head or skull. The Eskimo heads are higher and this trait is important because it excludes the Koniag Eskimos as important contributors to the evolutionary change that took place within the Aleut population. In this respect, child-rearing habits are sometimes influential. The Aleut did not flatten or otherwise deform the heads of their infants, as was done on Kodiak Island. The Aleuts used a soft cradle and there is no evidence of head flattening.

The cause of head broadening, a common trend over most of the world, has as yet no certain explanation. It is a growth change, manifested early in infancy, and its causes are undoubtedly mediated by many factors including early mother and child nutrition. Head broadening is also correlated with population density and evolutionary history. One speculation suggests that it is related to stress. Narrow

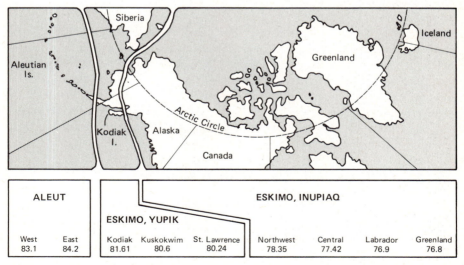

ALEUT		ESKIMO, INUPIAQ			
		ESKIMO, YUPIK			
West	East	Kodiak	Kuskokwim	St. Lawrence	Northwest	Central	Labrador	Greenland
83.1	84.2	81.61	80.6	80.24	78.35	77.42	76.9	76.8

Fig. 3. Male cephalic indices by geographic and linguistic distribution. Cephalic indices vary clinically with major differences between major linguistic divisions (courtesy B. Frølich).

heads are found in related peoples at high latitudes, such as the Arctic Eskimos, and in Indians living at high altitudes in contrast to closely related Indians living at low altitudes.

Aleut similarities to the Eskimos as a whole suggest that they were at one time, perhaps 10,000 or more years ago, a single variable population distributed along the coast of the Bering Land Bridge from the area now indicated by St. Lawrence Island down to Samalga Pass. The skeletal record proves that they were distinct from each other by 4000 years ago, which suggests that Aleuts and Eskimos had been geographically separated a great deal earlier. They have been diverging for a minimum of 9000 years, using the Anangula occupation as the western headquarters of the ancestral Aleuts. Aleuts are not Eskimos, although they are more closely related to Eskimos than they are to Indians. They have their own ethnic identity. They have their own race, language, and culture.

LENGTH OF LIFE

Longevity is an important variable, along with population size, density, and distribution. It is a useful measure of human adaptation and it is demonstrably related to culture. The intellectual achievements of the Aleuts are related to their remarkably long lifespan.

In 1871, Alphonse-Louis Pinart met an aged Aleut man on Wosnesenski Island who remembered when the Russians arrived in the country and whose age he placed at 120 years. Even if we assume that he did not see the first Russians of 1741, but only the beginning investiture of the eastern Aleutians marked by Glotov's discovery of Umnak Island in 1759 and his return to Umnak from Kodiak Island (Eskimo) in 1764, this elderly Aleut was at least 107 years old. Such observations are important indicators, but are not scientific evidence and cannot stand up in court.

Fortunately, Veniaminov published tables of age at death for much of his 10-year residency on Unalaska, and these do demonstrate that several Aleuts lived beyond age 90, and that a significant proportion (20 percent) lived beyond 60 years of age. This data can be extended to pre-Russian times by the use of skeletons where age at death is estimated from vault suture closure, age changes in the pubic symphysis of the pelvis, from the dentition, and more recently, by a photon/osteon technique. From the skeletal data, and in later times from written records, a well-founded picture of Aleut longevity emerges.

TABLE 2.2   POPULATION DENSITY

Isolate	Area km²	Number of Aleuts	Density of Aleuts	Number of Sea Otters	Density of Sea Otters
West	844	1,000	1.18	4,150	4.92
Central	3,200	5,000	1.56	15,500	4.84
East	8,725	10,000	1.15	42,100	4.82
Total	12,769	16,000		61,750	
Mean Density			1.253		4.836

One way of presenting longevity data is by means of population pyramids or survival curves. Figure 4 shows the population pyramid for Fox Island Aleuts, Commander Island Aleuts, and for the Sadlermiut Eskimos of Hudson Bay. The Aleuts are long-lived and the Eskimos are short-lived. At the same time, it appears that fewer children from birth to and including age four died in the eastern Aleutians compared with the Sadlermiut Eskimos of Southampton Island in Hudson Bay.

Childhood survivorship has many genetic, nutritional, and cultural components. The Aleuts avoided inbreeding, which removed one of the genetic contributions to infant mortality. Their nutritional intake was generally good. Nutritional deficiencies can occasionally be seen in the form of pitted lines in the enamel structure of the teeth (enamel hypoplasia). None of these are present in a small sample of children's skeletons from Amchitka Island in the central Aleutians. The Aleuts expended much time and ingenuity in caring for their children and this supervision undoubtedly contributed to the low mortality rate. Their knowledge of medical treatment, how to deal with breech deliveries, and how to remove a placenta may also have made a tangible contribution to the reduction of infant mortality.

As a consequence of living into the fifth and sixth decade of life, the risk of arthritis became greater. It is rare to see an Aleut skeleton of an individual over 40 years of age that is free of arthritis, especially in the spinal column and in the elbow.

A similar population profile of longevity and low infant mortality based on age of death of the cave burials of Kagamil Island is shown in Chapter 8. Thus it is apparent that Aleuts were long-lived before the arrival of the Russians as well as in the later period for which there is good data.

Another way of presenting data on length of life is by means of life expectancy analysis, a method used by insurance companies and researchers that must compare data from different groups living under different circumstances, and who must compare successive changes within the same group in different time periods. Life expectancy, based on life tables, permits the construction of informative tables for the ages where good data exists and does not require data for all periods of life,

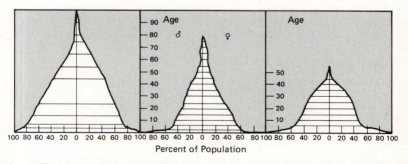

Fig. 4. Profile of populations of Aleuts of the Fox Islands (Unalaska Island, 1822–1836; data from I. Veniaminov, 1840), Commander Islands (1902–1917), and of the Eskimos of Southampton Island of Hudson Bay (until 1903; data from W. Laughlin, 1963; courtesy of Rychkov and Sheremetyeva, 1972).

although the accuracy and predictive power of such tables is improved by more and better data. Several tables for Aleut and Eskimo skeletal and living populations have been constructed by A. B. Harper (see Table 2.3).

The major parameters for different points in time are given in Table 2.3. Thus at age 10, an Aleut living during the Russian period might expect to live another 29.26 years; at age 50 he might expect to live another 12.52 years; and at age 80 he could expect to live two years or more. During the American period (for example in the year 1897 for which there was a reliable census), an Aleut male in the Aleutian chain at age 15 could expect to live another 29.56 years; at age 55 he might expect another 8.87 years; and at age 80 he could expect to be among the deceased. Age 15 is cited because this was the year before Aleut males began their life at sea, at which time drowning, marriage, and other hazards complicated their lives. The beginning of the age class is used for skeletal and mortality data, and the midpoint of the age class is used for census data.

The Pribilof Islands, St. Paul and St. George, lie 300 kilometers north of the Aleutian chain. These two islands are the principal breeding grounds of the fur seal. They were discovered by Aleuts, although they were apparently not inhabited prior to the Russian discovery in 1786 and the later permanent occupancy of them. In Aleut, they were known as "The Land-Uncle," and one of the Aleut heroes who landed there was "Ivory-Smasher." The first permanent occupation began under the Russians with the relocation of eastern Aleuts. The Pribilofs provide a poignant example of the relation between nutritional deprivation and life expectancy. The

TABLE 2.3   LIFE EXPECTANCY, MALE ALEUTS

Date	0–9	10–19	20–29	30–39	40–49	50–59	60–69	70–79	80+
Precontact period in Aleutian Chain									
Paleo-Aleuts	N.D.	35.77	27.56	21.22	15.00	9.29	5.00	N.D.	N.D.
Neo-Aleuts	N.D.	31.24	24.97	18.92	13.63	8.97	5.00	N.D.	N.D.
Average		33.51	26.27	20.07	14.32	9.13	5.00		
Russian period in Aleutian Chain									
1820–1829	35.50	32.73	26.65	21.67	17.55	15.65	14.41	9.55	5.00
1830–1839	34.52	32.42	26.06	22.69	17.19	13.29	11.58	8.89	5.00
1840–1849	24.81	27.38	24.13	20.64	14.60	10.32	8.16	5.00	0.00
1850–1859	20.57	25.98	21.44	19.49	16.52	10.83	9.00	5.00	0.00
1860–1869	20.22	27.81	23.08	17.38	16.67	12.50	7.00	5.00	0.00
Average	27.12	29.26	24.27	20.37	16.51	12.52	10.03	6.69	2.00
American period in Aleutian Chain									
1897	31.39	29.56	22.95	17.05	12.29	8.87	5.00	0.00	0.00
1948	32.30	25.17	26.09	22.87	15.84	10.29	5.00	0.00	0.00
Average	31.85	27.37	24.52	19.96	14.07	9.58	5.00	0.00	0.00
Pribilof Islands									
1870–1879	15.34	24.76	19.55	14.20	10.33	6.43	5.00	0.00	0.00
1880–1889	20.47	26.10	18.98	14.84	10.64	8.75	5.00	0.00	0.00
1897	21.92	25.10	18.75	15.00	10.71	8.33	5.00	0.00	0.00
1907	25.68	19.59	18.48	15.67	12.78	5.00	0.00	0.00	0.00
Average	20.85	23.89	18.94	14.93	11.12	7.13	3.75	0.00	0.00

people there do not live as long as their genetic relatives in their homeland, a short distance to the south.

In 1887, the Treasury agent for St. Paul Island prepared a list of the men who participated in the seal catch of 1870 (Table 2.4). Of these, no fewer than 46 of 68 died in this 17-year period. One man is identified by age and condition: "A confirmed invalid, very old (sixty-six years), oldest man on St. Paul Island." In contrast, a man of 66 in the Aleutian Islands would not be considered old, nor would he be the oldest survivor.

The life expectancy table (Table 2.3) provides a better quantified picture.

TABLE 2.4   FUR-SEAL FISHERIES OF ALASKA: ROLL OF NATIVES OF ST. PAUL ISLAND WHO SHARED IN THE SEAL CATCH OF 1870.
[Annotated July 1, 1887.]

No.	Name	Remarks
1	Artamanoff, Kerick	Healthy, but getting old.
2	Artamanoff, Herman	Dead.
3	Arkashoff, George	Dead.
4	Anulenock, Eupheme	Dead.
5	Avela, Marka	Dead.
6	Butrin, Kerick	Unable to do heavy work.
7	Butrin, Karp	Able man.
8	Bachoff, Michael	Dead.
9	Bolockshin, Benedict (1st)	Dead.
10	Bolockshin, Benedict (2d)	Dead.
11	Bezazihoff, Joseph	Healthy, but getting old.
12	Bezazihoff, Yevlampia	Dead.
13	Belaglazoff, Stephen	Dead.
14	Evanoff, John	Dead.
15	Evanoff, Tomothy	Dead.
16	Evanoff, Gabriel	Dead.
17	Glotoff, Timothy	Dead.
18	Hopoff, John, sr	Dead.
19	Kotchutin, Mark	Dead.
20	Kotchutin, Eupheme	Not able to do heavy work.
21	Kotchutin, John	Dead.
22	Kotchutin, George	Able man.
23	Kotchutin, Jacob	Able man.
24	Krukoff, Stephen	Dead.
25	Krukoff, Peter	Able man.
26	Kushin, Yermoli	Dead.
27	Kotchurgin, Gabriel	Dead.
28	Kozeroff, Michael	Dead.
29	Kuznitzoff, Pemen	Able man.
30	Kosloff, John	Dead.
31	Kematchnock, Philip	Dead.
32	Mandregin, Luke	Dead.
33	Mandregin, Eracklee	Dead.
34	Mandregin, John	Dead.
35	Mandregin, Jacob	Dead.
36	Meseekin, Perry	Dead.

TABLE 2.4 (*continued*)

No.	Name	Remarks
37	Nenarazoff, Alex	A confirmed invalid, very old (sixty-six years), oldest man on St. Paul Island.
38	Nocack, Myron	Dead.
39	Paranchin, John	Dead.
40	Pohomoff, Joseph	Dead.
41	Pancoff, Alexander	Dead.
42	Peeshenkoff, Peter	Healthy, but getting old.
43	Sedick, Zachar	Dead.
44	Sedick, Keer	Dead.
45	Sedick, Theodore	Able man.
46	Sedick, Dennis	Dead.
47	Sedick, Philip	Dead.
48	Suaroff, Paul	Dead.
49	Sutyagin, Antone	Dead.
50	Sutyagin, John	Dead.
51	Sutyagin, Jacob	Dead.
52	Squartzoff, Stephen	Dead.
53	Shabolin, Cæsar	Healthy, but feeble-minded and old.
54	Sedule, Vicele	Healthy, but getting old.
55	Tarakanoff, Platon	Dead.
56	Tetoff, Philat	Able man.
57	Viatkin, Demetrius	Dead.
58	Volcoff, Philip	Dead.
59	Volcoff, Markel	Able man.
60	Viatkin, Yevlampia	Able man.
61	Yatchmanoff, John	Able man.
62	Yatchmanoff, Nekita	Dead.
63	Haberoff, Paul	Healthy, but not strong.
64	Kruoff, Nicholas	Able man.
65	Krukoff, John	Dead.
66	Kushin, Aggius	Able man.
67	Shæsnikoff, Zachar	Dead.
68	Zaharoff, Yevmania	Feeble and worthless.

Recapitulation

Dead	46
Able men	15
Healthy old men	6
Confirmed invalid	1

From *Fur-Seal and Other Fisheries of Alaska*. Report from the Committee on Merchant Marine and Fisheries of the House of Representatives, 1889.

During the first 50 years of American supervision, life expectancy at age 15 averaged 19.2 percent less for Pribilof males than for Aleutian males. At other age cohorts, the deficiency of Pribilof Aleut life expectancy is considerably worse. Infant mortality is especially high and census profiles display an unusual lack of Pribilof Aleuts over age 70.

While the nutritional resources of the Pribilof Islands were excellent for millions of fur seals, and although the resident whites were not subject to high mortality, the Pribilof Islands were not as suitable an environment for sustaining a community of hunters as the Aleutians. This fact may be the principal reason that the Aleuts did not permanently occupy the Pribilofs before they were relocated there. The Pribilofs are colder than the Aleutians, and there are neither fresh water streams emptying from lakes (which are necessary for salmon), nor protected bay and reef systems. The islands are isolated (even more than Attu Island), there are only two important offshore islands, there is little driftwood, and the fur seals prevent collecting the major invertebrates. There are, of course, many attractive aspects: sea lions, abundant bird life, especially of cliff-nesting birds, and formerly, some sea otters, walrus, and fox. Halibut fishing is good, but there are few good boat landings compared with Umnak, Unalaska, or Akutan.

In the Aleutians, old men over 70 spent much time fishing from a two-hatch baidarka or from a baidar. They caught far more halibut and cod than they could possibly eat and were, therefore, important economic providers for others as well as for themselves. With increasing age, they fished more inside large bays and protected waters. Atka, Nikolski, Unalaska, and Akutan all have well-protected waters within bays and between small offshore islands. The limited number of places for launching and landing in the Pribilofs stands in marked contrast to the Aleutians. Today, the dory, which is more difficult to launch because of its weight, and to some extent skiffs still are used in significant numbers by older men for fishing.

How long a person ought to live is a speculative question. Most people want to live as long as they possibly can. Aleut culture abounds with charms and practices for living a long life. The Aleuts differed from the Eskimos in the health and medical practices they employed for living longer, in their nutritional base, and in the proportion of people who actually lived longer. The considerable longevity of the Aleutian and Commander Island Aleuts, comparable to that of the colonial settlements of the United States of 1776 and even later, stands out as an important biobehavioral characteristic. It composes an achievement that was both biological and cultural. It is not possible to say that the Aleutian Aleuts lived too long, but it is possible to say that the Pribilof Aleuts did not live long enough.

POPULATION DECLINE

The overall population of Aleuts has been estimated at 16,000 by several investigators. Of these, 10–11,000 were eastern Aleuts (Fox Island District), 4–5000 were central Aleuts, and 1000 were western Aleuts (Near Islands). Veniaminov estimated some 12–15,000 eastern Aleuts (excluding the Pribilof Islands), a figure that Hrdlička thought was probably too conservative, judging from the numbers and size of their former settlements. For the four or five centuries preceding 1741, a population of 10,000 Fox Island Aleuts is probably a valid estimate, although the number may well have been greater at various times.

In 1790 there were approximately 1900 Fox Island Aleuts. Thus the population experienced an enormous decline in only the 30 years between 1760 and 1790. It is possible that 50 percent of this reduction took place in the first 10 years of colonization, and that much of this reduction was concentrated in the years 1764–1768. Veniaminov, who talked to both Aleut and Russian participants, was inclined to believe that the number of Aleuts killed was in excess of 5000 rather than only 3000 as suggested by another chronicler. Glotov, Soloviev, and Pushkarev were apparently responsible for some 4000 deaths. The Russian Billings expedition of 1790 put an end to the earlier abuse, and an official investigatory expedition of 1768 probably had the effect of ameliorating the mistreatment. The court trials of offenders in 1764 undoubtedly helped to retard the killing.

On the other hand, an accurate estimate of the number of Russians killed at the hands of the Aleuts between 1760 and 1770 is not yet possible. Clearly, more than 100 Russians (including Kamchadals and Koryaks) were killed on Umnak and Unalaska, and possibly another 100 died as a consequence of starvation, disease, and drowning inflicted by Aleut attacks and prolonged sieges. Scurvy was the most common debilitating disease.

Starvation and disease continued to reduce the Aleut population beyond 1790 until an upward trend was established in the 1820s. One probable contributing factor to the high Aleut mortality in the Russian period was the fact that about 20 percent of the population was over 60 years of age. Old people, especially those over 70 years of age, do not respond well to dietary changes and relocation. This same loss of older people was noticeable when Aleuts from the central and eastern Aleutians were removed to relocation centers in southern Alaska during World War II, and when the western Aleuts of Attu were moved to Hokkaido by the Japanese. The earlier relocation of Aleuts to the Commander Islands appears to have been more congenial, and the population profile indicates that they lived approximately as long as the Aleut residents in the Aleutians.

Extensive and serious changes are taking place in the biology of the living Aleuts. Some diseases, such as tuberculosis and others that were a problem in 1948, have been brought under control by means of chemotherapy. When examined in 1948 the Aleutian Aleuts were generally lean and had only slight tendencies toward obesity. Restudy of Aleuts examined in 1978 shows an increase in obesity and in broadly-defined hypertension and heart disease. A recent study of St. Paul Island Aleuts indicates a prevalence of obesity and relatively high amounts of serum cholesterol and an increase in hypertension (Fig. 5). One village study in the chain in 1973 indicates a substantial increase in hypertension. It appears that as the people become more sedentary, and shift to a high-carbohydrate diet, they develop obesity, hypertension with resulting atherosclerosis, and its associated complications such as myocardial infarction, strokes, and heart failure. The 1948 study revealed very little hypertension, and heart problems generally were minor.

Dental and oral health have also declined. There has been a significant increase in decayed teeth, lost and extracted teeth, and in dental plaque in the 25 years between 1948 and 1973. Dental disease was relatively minor prior to the introduction of European foods, alcohol, and other dietary changes accompanying acculturation.

GROWTH RATE OF THE ALEUT POPULATION

The existence of 16,000 or more Aleuts at the time of their discovery can be fairly well documented. It is more likely to have been 17,000 than 15,000. But how

Fig. 5. Susan Beman, pipetting blood. A specimen of blood provides information for several studies dealing with heart disease, nutrition, genetics, and population affinities.

long had there been this many Aleuts? Do the figures accord with the natural resources, did sea cows become extinct, and were some animals, such as sea otters, in danger of becoming extinct? And if the Russians had not arrived, would the number of Aleuts have climbed even higher?

Many crucial factors depended on the technology and skills of the Aleuts. More whaling, more fur sealing, and more deep water halibut fishing could have added greatly to the food supply without endangering the supply of whales or halibut. In contrast, the population of sea otters and of sea lions theoretically could have been overhunted. It is possible that sea cows were killed off by the very first Aleuts. However, sea otters were not the major quarry until after the arrival of Russian fur hunters.

If we assume that 1000 Aleuts lived 9000 years ago, perhaps distributed in 10 or more villages from Anangula to Chagak to some point on the old Alaska Peninsula, we may then progress from 1000 to 16,000 Aleuts in several ways (see Fig. 6). The most likely model is very slow growth, with a possible increase in

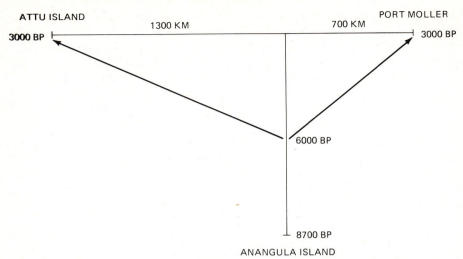

Fig. 6. Early Aleuts migrated in two directions from Nikolski Bay at the end of the Bering Land Bridge.

population growth rate soon after the major period in which the reef systems were exposed, some 5000 to 4500 years ago, and later, a return to a very slow growth rate (little above zero population growth). Approximately 1600 Aleuts were living 7–6000 years ago, 6000 were living 4–3000 years ago, and over 16,000 were living in 1741.

One of the mysteries of Aleut prehistory is the absence of old sites west of Samalga Pass. Although this may be because old sites exist but have not yet been found, it seems more likely that no major expansion took place before 4000 years ago, and the westward expansion from Samalga Pass was slow, taking 2–3000 years to reach the Near Islands with permanent, sustaining populations. An equally slow or slower migration or expansion rate pushed to the eastern boundary. A. B. Harper has cogently suggested that the eastward expansion was slower than that to the west because of the richer environment. Aleut population history illustrates a principle of general significance. Expansion is slower in areas of resource abundance; the environment is more adhesive than in areas of sparse resources.

The basis for this is Aleut fertility, combined with low infant mortality, which appears to be lower than that of Eskimos, although the evidence is incomplete and can scarcely be extended far into the past. It is likely that the Aleut population adjusted to the diverse natural resources in a demographically balanced form. Here, the data on length of life provides a valuable insight. Aleut longevity suggests a system that featured length of life rather than larger numbers with shorter generations and higher birth and death rates. The remarkable length of life of Aleuts proves to be an important factor in understanding their population history and their relationship to their environment as well. It is essential to understanding their sophisticated culture.

The fact that the antecedent populations of Aleuts can be studied by means of their skeletons has provided good evidence of the continuity of populations in the Aleutians. The dental traits in particular are the same in the living Aleuts as in their skeletal ancestors. Therefore, the Aleuts can prove that they are related to the skeletal population of Aleuts and that, historically, they have been the first and the only inhabitants of the Aleut domain. Their ownership is established by their skeletons and by the archeological context. They discovered their domain and dominated it.

3/Environment: the Aleut ecosystem

The Aleutian Islands are treeless, windswept, foggy, and volcanic. They appear to be barren, especially where land for hunters or farmers is concerned. To the Aleuts, these islands appeared to be an especially desirable place to live because they provided access to vast marine resources. The remarkable intellectual achievements of the Aleuts, their expert knowledge of human anatomy, manufacture of mummies, ability to count into high numbers with ease, art styles, and elaborate oral culture seem at first to be out of place in this harsh environment. How the Aleuts were able to construct a rich culture in this stressful area, and how the population was able to maintain and expand itself for several thousand years, is a fine example of human adaptability.

The explanation is by no means simple, but it is straightforward and logical. The intellectual achievements would not have been possible without a large and stable population base. The large population size, the genetic stability, the attainment of long life by many persons, and the low infant mortality, together with a high state of physical fitness, constituted the major prerequisites. A population with such characteristics would not have been possible except for the rich environment that the Aleuts cleverly and systematically exploited. These three elements, the intellectual achievements, the population size and stability, and the rich environmental potential were woven into a harmonious, mutually sustaining system.

The Aleuts used the islands as launching platforms from which they journeyed to extract their living from the coasts and the sea. The coastal areas were extremely rich in edible plants and animals: seaweeds, shellfish, birds, fish, sea otters, seals, and whales. The interior land surfaces, on the other hand, were irrelevant to their way of life. The islands could well be treeless, for the sea provided many kinds of driftwood from both Asia and America. The basketry grasses and land plants, an important addition to their varied diet, grew primarily along the coasts. The major base of the Aleut economic system was focused sharply on the sea.

Samalga Pass separates Umnak Island from the Islands of the Four Mountains to the west. This deep pass is located in a region that possesses one of the world's highest nutrient concentrations. It is a product of an inertial type of upwelling system that is caused by deep easterly currents from the Pacific sliding up the continental slope to cause surface outcropping. Other upwelling systems in the Aleutians, such as the one in Unimak Pass, are primarily wind driven and may shift from year to year. The importance of upwelling systems is that they promote vertical mixing of water, raising the basic nutrients into the upper sunlit zones where they become available to the great variety of life forms from microscopic supporting fauna to whales and, in turn, to the people who collect and eat the fish, birds, mammals, marine plants, and invertebrates. The Samalga Pass inertial upwelling system is of crucial importance to Aleut history because it was an ancient feature of the energy flow system and it made the Umnak area an especially rich area available to the Aleuts when they moved into the southwestern Umnak area.

The island passes channeled the migrating fur seals and whales, bringing them within range of the hunters. These passes are extremely turbulent. The currents, tidal bores, eddy systems, and rough seas imposed hazards on the kayak hunter, but they also promoted the rich nutritional system that supported the complex food chains ranging from the basic chemical components through phytoplankton, small and large fish, to the whales. Seen in this perspective, the Aleuts presided over the mixing of two great bodies of water, the Bering Sea and the Pacific Ocean.

The articulation of the elements of the culture, population, and environment composes an integrated ecosystem that must be analyzed to be appreciated. The relationship of the population to its environment is unique in many respects. It is instructive to see the way in which marine hunters have moved into a high reward–high risk area and have devised methods for exploiting the location far beyond the level of mere survival. The first prerequisite is a rich and stable environment. This environment is the foundation both for the success of the people and for their long and continuous occupation of the area.

DISTRIBUTION AND CHARACTERISTICS OF THE ISLANDS

From a worldwide perspective, the Aleutian Islands are volcanic outpourings along the southern rim of the North American plate, one of 12 rigid tectonic plates that make up the outer shell of the earth (lithosphere or mantle). Frequent volcanic activity, earthquakes, and the large number of volcanoes located in the Aleutian Islands reflect the enormous magnitude of heat generated and dissipated there as the Pacific plate slowly, but inexorably, moves under the North American plate. Tectonic uplift has continued to alter the coastline just as it did when the Aleutian Islands were originally raised above the sea millions of years ago.

The Aleuts occupied the western portion of the Alaska Peninsula and the slender chain of islands pointing toward the Kamchatka Peninsula of Siberia, which separated the Bering Sea on the north from the Pacific Ocean on the south. The total linear distance from east to west is 1250 miles (2000 kilometers), the longest longitudinal (east–west) distance occupied by a single language and racial group in the world. The eastern boundary of this domain was set at Port Moller on the north side of the Alaska Peninsula (in Bristol Bay) and at Kupreanof Point on the south side (in the Pacific Ocean) just east of the Shumagin Islands. Beyond this boundary line, approximately 160th meridian west longitude, the Alaska Peninsula was inhabited by Koniag Eskimos with whom the Aleuts traded and fought. The Koniags are better known for their possession of Kodiak Island where they attained, a large population of about 7000.

Much confusion has resulted from the Russian application of the term *Aleut* to the Koniag and Chugach Eskimos as well as to the Aleuts proper. The Aleuts themselves are amused by the fact that the Koniags may call themselves "Aleut," yet they cannot speak Aleut. The language, culture, and physical characteristics of the Eskimos are appreciably different from those of the Aleuts, and the term *Aleut* will be used here only for the Aleut speakers.

At the opposite end of their domain, the western boundary consists of over 180 miles (300 kilometers) of deep ocean separating Attu, the westernmost Aleutian island, from the two Commander Islands (Bering and Medni) of Siberia. These, in turn, lie 97 miles (155 kilometers) off the Kamchatka Peninsula. They are of special significance, because they appeared to be ideal stepping stones from Kamchatka to the Aleutians. However, they were uninhabited at the time of their discovery by Bering in 1741. The waters supported large numbers of sea mammals including the unique northern sea cow, extinct since 1768. The Commanders provide an example of the persistence of a rare species in the absence of human predation; additionally, the existence of the spectacled cormorant is evidence that there was no direct contact between Siberia and the Aleutians. Aleuts were moved to those two islands around 1826. Fewer than 200 live there now, and only on Bering Island at present.

The Aleuts are equally well insulated on both the north and south sides of their archipelago. The first islands to the north are the Pribilof Islands (St. Paul and St. George) lying approximately 260 miles (420 kilometers) north of Unalaska Island. They were occasionally visited, but not permanently occupied, by Aleuts prior to their discovery by the Russians in 1786. They are the major breeding ground for some 1.5 million fur seals who twice annually move through the Aleutian passes on their way to and from the Pribilofs. Over 600 Aleuts, drawn primarily from the eastern Aleutians, now live on the Pribilofs. Nearly 2000 miles (3200 kilometers) to the south are the Hawaiian Islands and other smaller islands, such as Midway, which serve as breeding grounds for three species of albatross, a bird of considerable importance to the Aleuts.

Thus Aleuts were isolated in an "appendix" where they were free to elaborate their own language and dialects and to evolve with a minimum of contamination from alien cultures and peoples. They shared only a small contact border with the Koniag Eskimos on the Alaska Peninsula. They were well buffered from the influence of American Indians by the intervening Eskimo populations.

CLUSTERING

There are about 100 islands in all. Except for the Shumagin Islands, lying immediately south of the Alaska Peninsula at the eastern end of the Aleut area, the Aleutian Islands are arrayed from east to west in a 900-mile (1450 kilometer) chain, with the larger islands clustered in the eastern portion. This land distribution has channeled movements of plants, animals, and humans with their diffuse cultural traits into a linear and longitudinal track. This pattern of distribution has influenced the pattern of social interaction. The practice of mummification originated in the eastern area and moved toward the west, but did not reach Attu, the end of the chain. Shape of the head, blood group genes, and other traits also have distributions suggesting that the diffusion of genes and culture traits alike has generally moved from the eastern Aleutians into the central and western islands.

Population density, dialect divisions, and the size, clustering, and complexity of the islands comprise an interdependent and coherent picture. A valuable insight into population dynamics, diffusion of cultural and genetic traits, and human migration emerges when time and direction factors are added. The demographic facts indicate that of the total 16,000 Aleuts estimated for the first year of European contact in 1741, 10,000 lived in the eastern Aleutians including the Alaska Peninsula and adjacent islands, 4–5000 lived in the central Aleutians, and only 1–2000 lived in the western Aleutians. This population distribution corresponds to the three major dialects of Aleut, the western or Attuan, the central or Atkan, and the eastern or Fox Island. These island divisions in turn have several subdivisions. The largest islands (Unimak, Unalaska, and Umnak) are found in the eastern Aleutians. The most westerly islands (Attu, Agattu, Shemya, Nizki, and Alaid) are known as the Near Islands because they were nearest to the Commander Islands and Kamchatka. They are separated by nearly 155 miles (250 kilometers) from the Rat Islands, the first subgroup in the central division. A small intervening island, Buldir, and a major reef system provided necessary aid to navigation, and acted as a rest-stop for skin-boat mariners, as well as being a village site.

Those physical features which affected the location of villages and camp sites, and thereby population density, include: coastline complexity (especially favorable are protected bays where fishing and collecting can be done during storms at sea); offshore islands (where seal and sea lions may haul up in rookeries); reef systems exposed at low tide (for the collection of sea urchins, octopus, seaweeds); tidal pools and lagoons (for shellfish and ducks); passes between the islands (which channel the movements of sea mammals and fish); lakes emptied by fresh water streams (where salmon rise to spawn); water depths (larger halibut are found in deeper water); currents (both fishing and the accumulation of driftwood are affected); beaches (sand or shingle beaches are easier to land on than rocky shores); cliffs (for nesting cormorants and puffins); proximity to an upwelling system; and of course, the local weather in general. The availability of plant foods and basketry grasses within walking distance of women was a related consideration.

From the Aleut point of view, the two overriding concerns were food supply in all its diversity—along with supply of fabricational materials—and accessibility of the foods and fabricational materials. An otherwise favorable location for a permanent winter village might be only a summer fish camp if constantly adverse winds or heavy seas made hunting and boat handling too difficult.

The eastern Aleutians were better endowed in terms of the features listed above and therefore had a larger population. More islands with complex coastlines, reefs, bays and islets, provide more ecological niches and, therefore, more species in greater abundance. Passes between the islands channel currents which enrich the water, particularly those passes connecting the Pacific Ocean and the Bering Sea. The tidal bores and currents flowing from the Pacific into the Bering Sea oxygenate the water, transfer nutrients, and are part of the upwelling system which enriches the upper water layers.

Still another benefit of islands with complex coastlines spaced only a few miles apart is the possibility of retrieval of whales and other animals which have been harpooned by hunters of one island but which have drifted while dying and then have been stranded on another island (Fig. 7). This unearned increment that accrues to a village that did not contribute to the hunting of the whale and that may be important to its economy is termed *external economy*. Not all whales harpooned by the whalers of one village were retrieved by the same village. While some of these were lost, others did drift ashore. These were added to the supply

Fig. 7. Author with skeleton of stranded whale, one of several beaked whales, Ilak Island, 1938. This small island had a permanent village and a mummy cave, and was abandoned soon after the Russian discovery. More recently it has been used for fox trapping (picture taken by Alan G. May or William Clemes, courtesy of the Smithsonian Institution).

of stranded animals, sea lions as well as whales, that died of natural causes and drifted ashore. Such stranded whales, whatever the original cause of death, represented a valuable food supply, oil for lamps, and bone for tools. Magical methods of great power were employed to insure that a stranded whale did not return to the sea. Even a small 20-ton whale could support a village of 50 persons for 800 days. This external economy increases correspondingly with the numbers of islands contiguous upon each other, the number of villages, the number of whalers, and appropriate currents and winds. While there is only one path between two islands, there are six paths between a cluster of four islands and fifteen paths between a cluster of six islands. The clustering of complex islands confers benefits on the social system by promoting simultaneous interaction between villages.

In brief, the physical features of the environment favor the increase of communities whose ability to extract more goods from the environment grows with the rise in the number of communities. The total population size increases by the multiplication of subunits which both directly and indirectly contribute to each other.

CLIMATE

The actual climate of the Aleutians seems incompatible with the magnificent meadows of flowers, droning bumblebees, and the ever-present sounds of birds. It is a wet, marine climate without great temperature extremes but with high winds and much fog. The most candid and authoritative statement on the weather is found in the Coast Pilot (1964: 343): "No other area in the world is recognized as having worse weather in general than that which the Aleutian Islands experience." Although the winds appear to be incessant and often of high velocity, there are occasional periods of calm. These brief remissions are recognized in the Aleut proverb, "the wind is not a river." The Aleuts are surely among the few, if not the only, people in the world to have a name for a social group based upon wind. There is a term or phrase, "in the lee of the house," for a cluster of men who watch the ocean from the leeward side of a house and who may discuss other matters than hunting while waiting for a seal to reappear or for a chattering of the surface—indicating that salmon are assembling for a run from the bay into the stream.

Winds have been clocked at 104 knots on Adak Island. Such winds have been seen to flip over airplanes, roll up metal landing strips, and drive large ships into reefs. Occasionally, a man will secure his house to the ground by means of a cable passing over the roof. Peculiarly, a high wind may wreak havoc on one side of an island while there is comparative calm only a short distance away on the opposite side. Williwaws are sudden and violent windstorms that frequently occur on the leeward side of mountains. The wind dams up on the windward side, then suddenly spills over and down the mountain side with remarkable force. It may bring precipitation with it or pick up surface water as it moves over the sea. Seen from the front, it may appear as a solid wall of water, dark and awesome.

The mean annual temperature is about 40° F. (5° C.) with August days rising to 70° F. (21° C.) and January days going down to 10° F. (−12° C.). The water is warmer than the air by a few degrees in the winter and slightly cooler than the air in the summer. Therefore, shore ice is rare and sea ice nonexistent. Practical consequences of open water the year round are reflected in the rich marine life. The cold water explains the continuation of childhood survival training practices designed to inure the person to cold. A rough estimate of the survival time of men immersed in these waters is less than half an hour. Aleut accounts of kayak accidents suggest that well-conditioned men could survive total immersion for as much as 45 minutes or more. Snowfall, like rainfall, varies greatly between islands and between villages on the same island. Adak Island averages only 17 inches (43 centimeters) whereas Atka, the next island to the east, averages 53 inches (133 centimeters).

4/Hunting

KAYAK HUNTING

Kayak hunting on the open sea is the most skilled and demanding form of hunting practiced by human beings. Kayak hunting was as important to the Aleut way of life as hunting in all its other forms has been for the successful evolution of the human species. Sea-mammal hunting placed the Aleuts squarely in the center of a high-reward area that at the same time carried high risks. The personal rewards for successful whaling or sea-otter hunting were considerable, both in this world and in the next. In this world they included acquisition of a large food and fabricational supply and social recognition that extended to an excellent funeral with provisions for a good life in the future world. More than this, there was a joy or pleasure in kayaking that sustained the hunter through incredibly adverse circumstances as well as the tedium of long voyages. Kayaking provided a time for thinking and for composing songs and stories. The goodness of fit between the Aleut and the kayak has been recorded in the aphorism that it was not possible to tell whether the kayak was made for the Aleut or the Aleut for the kayak.

There were many forms of hunting, but the most rewarding and dangerous kind was hunting on the open sea, out of sight of land, where navigational skills as well as physical prowess and accurate knowledge of animal behavior were prerequisites to success. A mishap to the skin boat or a sudden storm has drowned many skilled hunters. Each trip was a final examination for which the participants were placed in only one of two classes, the quick and the dead. Adaptation to the sea profoundly affected the psychology of the Aleuts, it quickened their minds and conferred rewards for mental acuity, and it exterminated the incompetents.

Hunting is a complex organization of behavior, and not simply a "subsistence technique." It includes considerably more than the dramatic killing of a sea lion or harpooning a whale. The methods of dispatch or killing are only a small, but necessary, part of the process. Man evolved as a hunter, he spent over 99 percent of his species' history as a hunter, and he spread over the entire habitable area of the world as a hunter. If man had not made the decisive step from a vegetarian diet to a meat diet, he would still be in the jungle with gorillas and chimpanzees, eating leaves and bamboo shoots. That man achieved a world-wide distribution while still a hunter reflects the enormous universality of this kind of behavioral adaptation. The major prerequisite is a knowledge of animal behavior and a knowledge of the appropriate behaviors in response. Harpoons, spears, arrows, and clubs are not usually effective at long ranges. The native hunter has to invest more in tracking and approach in order to use his killing weapons. In marked contrast, modern trophy hunters can dispense with a knowledge of animal behavior and stalking. Using a high-powered rifle with telescopic sights, an animal can be shot at a distance of more than 300 meters, and helicopters or light planes simplify the location and approach to game. Thus, the simplicity of technology of early man and primitive peoples does not mean a simple mind; it simply means that they invested more heavily in appropriate training and knowledge that lead up to the killing.

In hunting societies generally, and most prominently in Aleut society, hunting was an organizing activity with multitudinous physiological, psychological, social, genetic, and intellectual ramifications. These factors, which are often partitioned into separate disciplinary divisions, are of course unified in the individual. In recognition of their natural unity and their developmental continuity in the individual, they may be termed biobehavioral elements.

The total biobehavioral configuration of hunting includes the ethological training of children to be skilled observers of animal behavior, as well as that of other humans. The process includes five distinguishable components, each with special training and technological correlates: (1) childhood programming; (2) scanning or collecting information; (3) stalking and pursuing game; (4) immobilizing or killing game; and (5) retrieving game. Viewed against this schedule, Aleut kayak hunting has many unique elements and very broad ramifications in the total Aleut culture.

CHILD TRAINING FOR HUNTING AND SURVIVAL

The point at which Aleut training protocol differs from that of most other hunters lies in the specificity of the exercises. Running and wrestling are generally good preparation for active hunting. However, different people have somewhat similar exercise programs for the reasons that, aside from the activity itself, general exercises are adequate preparation. The Aleut hunter must sit for several hours in his kayak, feet outstretched in front of him, and paddle. From the kayak, he must throw a harpoon with a throwing board. It was advantageous, therefore, to actually stretch the ligaments and tendons of the knee, back, and shoulder, and for this to be done early in life.

One disarming example of an arm-twisting routine placed the uncle, father, or grandfather behind the seated child. The preceptor gently pulled the boy's arm straight over the shoulder and back behind the head. This was done intermittently and accompanied by a song or with susurrating sounds. Beginning as early as age one, this exercise made the shoulder joint supple and permitted a greater excursion from behind with a straight arm, a valuable ability for casting harpoons with the throwing board.

In another exercise, the child was seated on a box with his legs extended and heels resting on another box. The tutor then massaged his knees and pressed down on them gently, accompanying this treatment with a rhythmical sound, "t-t-t-t-." The boy was required to bend his foot and toes far forward, and then far backward. This exercise lengthened the hamstring muscles on the back side of the lower thighs and lower legs (*M. semimembranosus* and *M. semitendinosus*) and also loosened the muscles in the small of the back, thus enabling him to sit comfortably in a kayak. Aleuts commonly ridiculed the Koniag Eskimos because they knelt in their kayaks.

A third exercise saw the child hung by his fingers from a ceiling beam of the *barabara*. Only his fingers suspended him some five feet (1.5 meters) above the ground. Occasionally the child would begin to cry as though he was afraid he would finally drop to the grass-covered earth floor. Sometimes he landed on his feet, and sometimes on his seat, but then he would laugh. Pleasure in these exercises always reappears as a prominent feature. The child was instructed to land gracefully on his feet. A principal purpose of this training was preparation for climbing on cliffs so that, "even if he fell from high place he wouldn't be hurt inside." Gathering the eggs of puffins, murres, and cormorants required agility and tenacity in climbing on high, wet cliffs. Another object was, of course, to strengthen the fingers. A variant of this finger-hanging was being lifted by the head, and then by the feet, and then dropped. Like the other exercises, this was performed before breakfast.

Another kind of exercise consisted of finger squeezing. The boy's preceptor squeezed the four fingers of his hand until he and they turned pale. In this case, the point was to ensure that he had warm hands when he was an adult. Old men prided themselves on having warm hands and believed this kind of exercise was responsible for them.

A variety of games naturally reinforced the training and gave some specific training for kayak hunting. In one game, each of two opposing players sat on the ground facing each other, 12 feet (3.7 meters) or 15 feet (4.6 meters) apart, with feet straight out, as though sitting in a kayak. Beside each boy was a flexible wood withe or lath from which a small model of a whale was suspended. Each player took turns throwing a dart at the whale of his opponent. This game accustomed the boy not only to sitting with his legs outstretched, but to performing a skilled maneuver at the same time. By the time the boy was ready for kayak instruction, around age 10, he commanded the appropriate postures and endurance, and could focus his attention on learning to balance the boat, maneuver, cast harpoons, and navigate. All the while he was of course observing the habits of animals and receiving information on weather prediction, water conditions, tidal changes, and fabricational techniques.

"Strong Man" training was a specialized extension of the typical boy's training. All strong men did not command the title of Strong Man, but all those titled Strong Man were undeniably strong. Not all Aleut boys underwent this special training because it involved the development of power that was spiritual as well as physical and invariably resulted in the premature death of the Strong Man. The association of great power with the penalty of premature death is a recurrent theme in Aleut culture. The boys were expected to get up at dawn, before the sun rose, and bathe in the ocean or in running water. Only the face remained above the water. They were then expected to exercise. A particularly stressful exercise was running uphill carrying stones. The size of the stones was increased as the boys prospered under this regime. The tutor watched them carefully, listened to their hearts, and observed their breathing after such runs. In addition to historical and legendary accounts of strong men, there are some examples known to qualified observers. A machine for testing hand grip (dynamometer) employed by anthropologist W. J. Jochelson in 1910 was damaged by one very strong Aleut who bent the registering needle by squeezing beyond the maximum. Another man in Nikolski was seen lifting an 18-foot (5.5 meters) dory. Powerfully developed skeletons attest to the great strength of some individuals in the past. The considerable curvature of the vertebral border of the shoulder blades (*scapulae*) in male skeletons in particular reflects the development of the shoulder and arm muscles.

Although the list of things a boy should not eat was extensive, the variety of foods available made these restrictions very light. More important than avoiding fish tails, which would make him tremble like the tail of a fish in motion, was the proscription on eating after dark. The last meal was eaten during the daylight and the boy went to bed early. The explicit rationale for eating during the day reposed in the logic that if you ate at night you might get grass in your food. This was displeasing to the sea mammals who easily detected such noxious substances as grass and also women's hair.

An associated belief was contained in the rule that the young boy must not "walk at night." The stated reason was reasonable but served quite another function. This is a polite euphemism for visiting women. If the boy walked at night, he might get grass on his feet, which would surely offend the sea mammals. One charming story tells of an unsuccessful hunter who had been walking at night. Finally, after a long period of failure, a friendly octopus cleaned his hands, feet, and the inside of his stomach, each with a separate tentacle. This restored him to the good graces of the marine mammals, and he became a successful hunter. Inside the village, the proscription on "walking at night" served the important function of reducing competition between men and boys for the favors of females. This delightful euphemism is typical of the diplomatic guidance given to young people.

Even the sleeping habits of the boy were supervised; he was never permitted to sleep on his back, and he should be ready to leap into action at any time. Examples of the "old people," the *kadangin* of pre-Russian times, were frequently cited. They, the forebears of the people, always slept with one arm in the air. If it fell down, they immediately awakened. In this way, they could never be surprised by an enemy seeking to kill them.

One Aleut who had the traditional hunter's child training recalled that when he killed his first seal, his father took out the heart, still spurting blood, and had him eat a piece of it. Much of the food was eaten raw, especially by hunters on trips where the young boys were tutored in the best ways of doing things.

About age 10, a boy might be permitted or encouraged, depending upon his maturational status, to experiment with a kayak in a lake or even along the shore if the bay was calm. An adult was present to advise and encourage. In each case orders and directions were never shouted. The boy was encouraged to get the feel of the boat. This is still done with dories in the bay. It was intended always to be a pleasant experience and to increase the boy's familiarity with the boat and, importantly, his own feeling of competence.

At age 13 or 14, the boy began to hunt with his uncles or father. Between age 16 and 19, the boy had his own *baidarka* (kayak) and might undertake trips on his own. By then he was also capable of making his own boat frame and of persuading some women to sew skins for him. A young man capable of persuading three or four women to sew for him was obviously prepared to cope with sea lions and whales.

Another aspect of child training deserves mention because it had many functions. The equipment, especially the throwing board and the practice spears, had to be fitted to the individual. The throwing board of one person could not be used by another person since its length was determined by the distance from his middle finger to his elbow. One Aleut pointed out that this made stealing unremunerative. Children practiced throwing spears on land long before they hunted from a kayak. They practiced in games and on birds. Although sea otter hunting was prohibited by law in 1911, and rifles were used for seals and sea lions, the children continued the use of throwing boards and spears. In our 1938 visit to an Aleut village, we were greeted the first day with the sight and sound of boys moving through the village casting spears at birds and rabbits. They also continued the use of the crossbow, a Russian introduction, as a toy capable of shooting birds. In each case, the child owned his own equipment. They were his personal possessions for which he alone was responsible and he was the only person who could transfer ownership. The Aleut attitude toward private property was ingrained early and effectively. Private ownership was, and still is, an operating value system.

The physical and technological training of the boy was accompanied all the while by tutored training in the observation of animal behavior (ethology—not to be confused with ethnology). Since this depended upon observation, the emphasis was placed upon disciplined observational abilities. The child should observe the age changes in each animal and bird, their food preferences, their flying or swimming attitudes, and their responses to other animals. Their behavior in relation to time of day and weather conditions was particularly important. Pets were commonly kept and used to great advantage. A gull on a string could be tested with various foods and for amount of food. The child learned what made him vomit and what he preferred to eat and what amounts to feed him at any one time. The same applied to eagles, ravens, geese, and ducks, and occasionally, a young seal. Since each bird has a flight distance, which he is likely to betray, it was important to learn how close to a bird the hunter can approach, in order to get the best possible shot, before the bird will fly off. A shift in balance or a grouping of a bird's muscles may betray its intent to fly off. Thus keen observation meant the difference between a good shot and a poor one, or none at all. Each boy became conversant with the entire inventory of birds, mammals, and fish as well as invertebrates (especially octopus). The knowledge of ethology that an adult male accumulates is astounding.

At the same time, the habit of acute observation was extended to include humans. The child learned by observation when to address an adult and when to avoid one. The set of the face, the pulsing of the temporal artery, the set of the lips, all were observed. The ability of the Aleuts to mimic visitors rests firmly on their training in animal behavior.

LOCATING GAME

The second step in the sequence pattern of hunting is locating the game. This is done by scanning in a likely area. Seated in his light craft, the hunter could scan a minimal area over two miles (3.2 kilometers) in radius or more, depending upon the height of waves. For searching along an indented coastline and nosing inside bays and lagoons, the kayak hunter had the great advantage that inspection of the shoreline could be carried out without retracing the route. The hunter could circle inside a bay, inspecting both sides and moving to any one point with ease where the sound of exhausting lungs or a disappearing flash of brown hinted that a seal was present. The silence of the kayak and its lack of offensive odor were important to searching sweeps before the hunt began.

Another advantage of the kayak hunter over the foot-slogging land hunter depends upon the submarine topography. Moving out from the shore and over a deep pass, he glides over canyons, cliffs, and steep hills, each possessing its own animal communities. He passes over these in quick succession while traveling only a short horizontal distance. It is more economical to drop a hook and line 200 feet (60 meters) down to a halibut than to climb 200 feet up a mountain side for almost any kind of quarry. Many whales habitually remain in deep water. They go to the canyon bottoms for their feeding but must return to the surface for air. Mountain goats, sheep, or brown bears are under no similar compulsion to come down to the foot of their mountains. In this sense, the kayak hunter is a horizon hunter and takes advantage of the fact that all sea mammals must return to the surface at some point to breathe. He samples more ecological zones more quickly, he scans efficiently, and if game is in the area, the Aleut hunter is likely to find it.

STALKING AND PURSUIT

Once game has been located by scanning, the next step—getting close enough to spear it—becomes the tactical problem. The approach may be slow and tedious if the day is clear and the sea is calm, for sea mammals can pick up sounds at great distances both above and below water. Once alerted, they promptly identify an odd shape or odor. For small mammals, such as seals and sea otters, the maximum effective range for a light harpoon (4-foot length, 1.2 meters) that is thrown with the aid of the throwing board, is 120 feet (36.6 meters). Although this distance is well attested to in historical accounts and by Aleuts, it must be emphasized that it is a maximum distance.

Following a single animal may require hours. Several hunters might form a circle and hasten the exhaustion of a sea otter by forcing him to dive quickly each time he surfaces. Stalking in storms or rough seas has the advantage of damping sound and odor as well as providing cover in the troughs of waves, but harpoon throwing is much more difficult. Fog provides a useful cover, although the sound of a dripping paddle or slap of water on the kayak might alert the quarry.

The hunter can maintain a velocity of four knots for long periods, and more than double this for short spurts. Seals can thereby be winded by the hunter, for they can seldom remain below more than 15 or 20 minutes, and much less on successive dives when they are harried. Sea lions present a more formidable problem, for they might turn on the hunter; whales have the same discomforting habit. However, the most aggressive animals are docile as vegetables when asleep. The kayaker, if he did not first spear the animal, might follow him at a distance for several hours on the chance of catching him napping; or in the case of the pinnipeds, of stalking the prey to the point where they haul out on a rock for rest and sleep.

KILLING

Killing or otherwise immobilizing the animal is most frequently described in accounts of Aleut hunters, even though this phase is necessarily preceded by the steps that require as much or more instruction and experience. For small mammals, such as sea otters and seals, it is more often an anticlimax. A light harpoon with a float attached to the shaft, or a float on the end of the line, or simply the shaft itself as a drag, is sufficient to slow the animal so that the kayaker can lance or club the animal. More animals have been dispatched by a club than any other weapon known. A blow above the ear in the parietal region is adequate for most pinnipeds and sea otters but not for walrus and whales. Sea mammals sink, and if somewhat undernourished, they may sink soon after being wounded. The genius of the harpoon is simply that it provides a means of puncturing the animal and of attaching a line, so that he is slowed down whether he is bleeding seriously or not. The line on the animal permits the hunter to get close to the prey to dispatch him if he is still alive and to retrieve him if he has sunk. Sea mammals are not ordinarily killed by harpooning. The use of guns has resulted in large losses of sea mammals, sometimes 50 percent of those shot. The efficiency of the kayak and the harpoon must be measured by the percentage of successful retrievals after the hit has been made.

RETRIEVAL

This part of the hunting process is, again, well served by the nature of the kayak. Unlike a trophy hunter, the Aleut had to deliver the carcass to the cooks in order to collect his awards. The largest of each species was not ordinarily appreciated either by the hunter or by the cook. A large bull sea lion is difficult to approach, difficult to kill, difficult to carry back home, and difficult to eat. His hide may be badly scarred from fights with other sea lions, usually over his dominance of a portion of a rookery and a harem of cows. The same energy expended on three young sea lions is more rewarding in terms of reduced hazards, better meat, and more fabricational materials of skin, flippers, intestines, throat, and sinew. Having secured his sea otter or sea lion, the hunter might tow it home, or he might land nearby to cut up the animal, stow it inside the kayak (especially if the boat is a larger two-hatch kayak), and take it home. In the case of a small harbor seal, female fur seal, or sea otter, the animal might simply be lashed to the deck. Whales were towed by several hunters in tandem.

If an animal sinks in reasonably shallow water and the float or shaft is lost, the hunter uses a retrieving hook for grappling.

The versatility of the kayak becomes evident again in its ability to tow or carry several hundred pounds of meat to the village. The kayak is made more efficient than transport over land because most of the weight of the dead animal is borne by the water. In marked contrast, land hunters enjoy no such dividend; they must move the total weight by their own efforts. For Eskimos who use sleds, the efficiency of weight borne on runners does not approach that of natural flotation, and dogs that are used to drag the sled eat nearly as much as the people who are to be fed by what is left. The sled hunter must hunt to feed his team, which otherwise will not function or might feed upon him. The Aleut hunter does not have to feed his kayak; at most it takes only a little water.

THE KAYAK AND HUNTING EQUIPMENT

The supreme technological achievement of the Aleut was his kayak, and the skillful use of this light skin boat represented a well-scheduled child-training program. In Aleut the kayak is termed an *ikyak* or *ikyaadak*, the latter meaning a small or little umiak and a word derived from the old word for an umiak, *ik*. The most commonly used term, however, is *baidarka*, a Siberian word introduced by the Russians. The large open skin boat known in Eskimo as *umiak* was also designated by a Russian word, *baidarra*, or simply *baidar* in two of its most commonly rendered forms. The chiton was also termed a *baidarka*. The origin of the kayak cannot be determined, although the above terminology suggests that it is a derivative of an open and more cumbersome skin boat. It was probably invented by ancestral Aleuts who enjoyed the necessary prerequisites: open water, wood, the use of some kind of skin-covered boat, and the motivation of tangible and immediate rewards for a waterproof boat that could be launched through the surf and used in heavy seas. Archeological evidence, however, is lacking. The inventory of faunal remains at Chaluka and Anangula village suggests that it was already in use at the beginning of that phase of Aleut occupation. The pelagic albatross, fur seal, and whale bones point to the early use of kayaks by prehistorical Aleuts.

There were many kinds of kayaks; more variant forms were used by the Aleuts than by any other people who used kayaks. They were made in one-hatch, two-hatch, and, after the arrival of the Russians, in three-hatch forms (Figs. 8, 9, and 10). The administrator occupied the middle hatch. They varied greatly in length. A small one-hatch form was as short as 13 feet (4 meters) in length and weighed only 30 pounds (13.6 kilograms). In all Aleutian forms the bow is cleft and assumes either an erect position or a horizontal position. The horizontal cleft is known to be only an Aleutian style and it appears to have disappeared from use during the Russian period. The vertical cleft form became dominant for both single- and two-hatch variations. This bow form is explicitly stated to emulate a sea otter characteristically lying on its back, its arms in front of its head. The shouldered stern is made only by Aleuts.

An ingenious part of the basic design was the use of a two- or a three-piece keelson, the main member running down the bottom inside length of the boat (see Fig. 8). The three pieces were joined with angle cuts and firmly lashed together with baleen. A shim of polished ivory or bone might be inserted at the matching faces of the three pieces to prevent wear on the wood and to improve flexion. This invention provided a high degree of flexibility and prevented fracture of the main

Fig. 8. *Atka, 1948. Model of single-hatch* baidarka *with middle section of three-piece keelson not yet installed.*

Fig. 9. *Nikolski, 1948. Aleut men carrying two-hatch* baidarka *in shoulder position. Nikolski reef and Anangula Island can be seen in the background.*

Fig. 10. Mr. Sergei Sovoroff of Nikolski holds a three-hatch baidarka *model, with a rudder at the stern and a cleric in the middle hatch reading a book while the Aleuts paddle for him. Mr. Sovoroff is an elderly Aleut of considerable physical and intellectual vigor. Self-taught, he reads and writes Aleut and, with his wife Agnes Sovoroff, teaches the Aleut language.*

element. It facilitated traversing waves as well as resisting the extreme pounding in running through heavy surf and breakers.

The cover was usually made of sea lion skins, four or five for a small kayak. All the ribs and long members, hatchcombing, and bow piece were neatly rounded, polished, and often painted red. The ribs were steamed, for which one interesting technique was to place the rib inside a length of kelp. Aleut kayak makers also held the rib in their teeth while they shaped it for proper curvature. The skins were cut to shape by men, sewn by women, pulled over the frame by the men, and the remaining long slit behind the hatch was sewn or laced by men. The skin was usually replaced each year, although it could be taken off and stored separately from the skeleton if the *baidarka* was left on a rack during the winter. The women who did the sewing had to bind their hair and be especially careful not to get hair in a seam, for a sea lion would bite out that portion and cause the death of the hunter.

Paddles were double-bladed and sharply pointed. Occasionally, the points were tipped with ivory so that the paddle could be used as a lance. Other things essential to the boat included a drip skirt that was permanently attached to the hatchcombing. The hunter pulled it up under his arms and tightened it with a drawstring. A single suspender passed over the left shoulder of right handed men. Ballast stones carried inside the boat were named "sea lion stones" after the stones carried in the stomachs of sea lions.

Inside the *baidarka*, the hunter usually had a bailing tube, a long cigar-shaped wooden tube made of two half-tubes lashed together (Fig. 11). With this, the hunter could suck up water inside the boat by holding the tube between his legs, then covering the lower end with one finger. He then emptied the water in the tube over the side of the kayak with one hand. Patching material was always included for sharp rocks and irrascible sea lions were a constant hazard. A flat rock or piece of wood was inserted between the skin and the frame of the kayak to plug small holes. A little blubber was usually available for daubing and could be used for many other purposes. In cold weather, if the hunter needed to make a fire on snow or very wet ground, he could take the dry grass from inside his boots, pound it into the blubber, and start a fire with wet wood.

Accidents overtook the hunters in spite of the best precautions. Most serious at sea was a large tear or fracture of the frame with too large a hole to plug. Hunters usually had a partner (a formalized relationship) with whom they hunted on overnight trips or under hazardous conditions. The partner picked up the sinking hunter and carried him to shore. If a two-hatch *baidarka* sank, the two hunters joined hands over the deck of the rescuing craft for the trip to shore. If caught in the open sea by a williwaw or a prolonged storm, several hunters would lash their *baidarkas* together, thus forming a multihulled craft with sufficient flexibility to ride out a storm that would sink a single boat. This technique was also employed by a raiding party. They hoped to be mistaken for a floating kelp bed long enough to get close enough to make an effective landing. The Aleuts have a word specifically for this kind of cluster of kayaks.

The personal dress of the hunter consisted first of his waterproof parka (*kamleika*), made of intestine or throat (esophagus). Its hood could be tightened about the face with a drawstring. The sleeves could be made watertight by bands tied on the outside around the wrists. Trousers and boots were optional. Although the *baidarka* itself and the *kamleika* were tastefully decorated with small feathers of eagles, cormorants, or puffins sewn into the seams and with fast pigments, the crowning glory of the hunter were his visor and his hat. Most commonly worn was the wood visor, beautifully painted with curvilinear designs in different colors and with the long whiskers of the sea lion projecting from the rear or from the

Fig. 11. Mr. Fred Bezezekoff emptying water from dory with bailing tube. This pump has been made in the larger size for the dory; a smaller one was used for the baidarka.

offarm side. A little ivory figure sometimes sat on the long sloping bill, and a twisted sinew line passed under the chin. The more elaborate full hat came to a peak and more often had hunting scenes depicted on its surface as well as painted designs. A long, carved ivory wing passed vertically up both sides of the hat, and the seam at the rear was covered with a strip of bone or ivory (Ivanov, 1928). These hats were made of wood, scraped thin, polished, and steamed into shape. Because of their length, a small wooden forehead rest was often glued on the inner surface. The visor and the full hat performed the valuable functions of keeping water out of the hunter's eyes and of reducing glare on sunny days. The full hat was used for ceremonial occasions, such as for formal visits between villages.

A belt knife of chipped stone hafted in a wood or bone handle was standard equipment on land or sea. A water bottle was carried on the deck behind the hatch. Some were made of wood, others from the pericardium (the external tissue sheathing the heart) of a sea lion or a brown bear. An amulet was, of course, a necessity.

Hunting gear was carried on the deck, tucked securely under thongs that ran across the deck, both fore and aft. The throwing board (*atlatl* is a commonly used term) was an extension of the arm, a carefully carved and painted wood billet that enabled harpoons and spears to be cast much farther than could be done by the arm alone. The butt of the spear was engaged by an ivory pin set in a shallow channel. Since it could be used with one hand, the other hand could be used to steady the *baidarka* by holding the paddle with one blade in the water. Bows and arrows were seldom used from single-hatch *baidarkas*, since they required two hands.

The Aleut throwing board, unlike all those used by Eskimos, had a hole for the index finger. The complex surfaces and angles can be best appreciated in the photographs (Fig. 12). Black paint on the back side represented the fur of the sea otter, and red paint on the belly represented blood. The various parts had anatomical names: the distal end, the belly side, was the "forehead." The ivory engaging pin was the "ziphisternum," and the basin for the palm of the hand was named for the palm of the hand.

Harpoons and spears were also carried on the deck. The basic sea otter harpoon

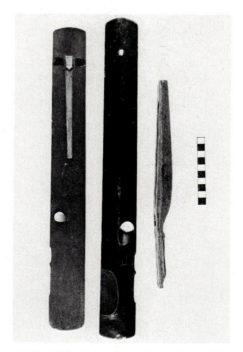

Fig. 12. Specimens of Nikolski Aleut throwing boards. The left specimen shows groove and ivory pin (ziphisternum) on front side (forehead is at top). The middle specimen shows back with place for palm of right hand and hole for index finger. The specimen at right is a child's throwing board in use in 1938.

was four feet (1.2 meters) in length. The ivory head sat in a wood-lined socket in the whalebone socket piece. Other detachable harpoon heads were larger, and each had its own two-piece wood case. A float, made of a whole sealskin with nubbins of the flippers obtruding, was carried behind the hunter. This was used for many things, from floating whales to decoying seals and, importantly, as a life saver.

Another basic item was a retrieving hook (see Fig. 13). This ingenious object had a wood shaft resembling a cigar but was slightly triangular in cross section. An iron halibut hook—probably made of bird bone or ivory in earlier times—was firmly lashed to the far end, and a small weight hung from the end on a short line. Attached to a long line, this retrieving hook could be cast from shore over the floating carcass of a seal and then drawn in. The shape of the shaft and the weight directed the hook into the carcass. It was invaluable for retrieving birds and even for catching salmon when they were running. Like a fishing line, sinker, and hook, it was not essential to hunting from a *baidarka*, but it was generally useful and was often carried on hunting trips. A club was an essential and unvarying item of hunting gear. Halibut and other fish, as well as sea mammals, were dispatched with this two-foot (0.6 meter) wood or whalebone club. A small lamp and other gear might be stowed inside if a long trip were planned.

A fully equipped hunter was a magnificent sight and was also a large investment in materials and man-hours of labor. It was important to present a pleasant appearance to entice the sea mammals to approach the boat, especially the sensitive sea otter. A powerful charm that was carefully wrapped in a waterproof pouch and that was known only to the hunter, in addition to many precautionary customs, were all necessary parts of open sea hunting. If a man slept with a woman, he must share the woman with the kayak who would otherwise become jealous, break, and not return the hunter to his village. This sharing consisted of rubbing the kayak in the morning before going out to sea. Interestingly, this practice was transferred

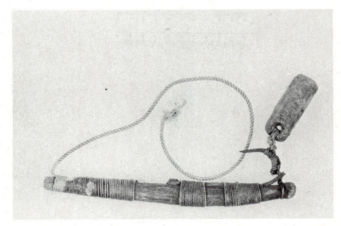

Fig. 13. Retrieving hook. It was used with fishing line of desired length, with a weight attached to the end beyond the hook. It was cast over the body of a sea lion or a seal to pull it back to shore. It was also used as a grappling hook for sunken sea mammals.

to the dory and continued into recent times. An old story vividly depicts the plight of a hunter who failed to share his woman with his kayak and perished within sight of his family who awaited his return.

Avoidance of women was always an important custom, as was the fear of carrying to the sea a land product, such as grass. Whales and sea otters could immediately detect any hunter who dallied with women and promptly avoided such an imprudent person. Sea lions, oddly, were apparently less discriminating. A one-month avoidance of woman was necessary before sea otter hunting but none for the sea lions.

WHALING

Of the six families of whales and dolphins accessible to the Aleuts during part or all of the year, the humpback whale was most commonly hunted. Whaling was done mostly in the spring of each year and continued into the summer. A large proportion of the whales entering the Bering Sea from the Pacific Ocean entered through the Aleutian passes. Some, such as the California gray whale, entered only through the eastern Aleutian passes. The flourishing whaling fleets of the Bering Sea and a former commercial station at Akutan attest to the abundance of whales.

After a whale had been sighted, according to an Unalaska method, the top whaler (*alananasika*) set out alone in a single-hatch kayak. He cast a light stone-tipped spear into the whale. Upon setting the spear firmly, the "killer" immediately returned to his village. He told the people where he had speared the whale and then went into seclusion in a small isolation hut. He did not eat, drink, or consort with women. He behaved instead like a sick man and thus, by sympathetic magic, attempted to persuade the whale to be sick. He remained in seclusion two or three days, depending on how long was required to retrieve the whale and bring it ashore. In the meantime, the village hunters maintained a watch on the whale. *Baidarkas* went after the whale and watched it as the spear worked its way deeper into the body. If mortally wounded, the whale eventually slowed down and finally began to turn in circles, making a labored "pooing" sound as it slowly expired. By this behavior, the watchers knew it was about to die.

For fear of having their boats broken by the whale, the Aleuts did not at first go near it. One man detached a point from a harpoon and hit the whale twice with the blunt end of the socketpiece. If it did not twitch, they then slit its upper lip and attached a line. Several *baidarkas*, arranged in tandem, cooperated to tow it ashore. The line passed from the whale to the hatchcombing of the first *baidarka*, from the first to the second and on to the last one at the head of the towline. If it was far to the village, floats would be attached to provide additional buoyancy. It was not always possible to get the whale back to the village, and many were lost entirely.

Upon reaching shore, a messenger was sent to tell the killer that the whale had arrived. The hunter who harpooned the whale then rose from his sick bed, came down to the whale, and cut out the place where the spear had gone in. This place was "swollen like a saucer turned upside down." The entire area, all the way to the bone, must be removed because it was considered poisoned. The killer then carried this section up onto dry land, dug a hole some five feet (1.5 meters) deep, jerked the spear out and dropped the contaminated portion into the hole. Properly enclosed, it could do no harm.

There is no substantial evidence that the Aleuts had or used a toxic poison. Rather, their poisons appear to have been magical in nature. One "poison" consisted of bumblebee legs, a big black beetle, and a little shrimp-like isopod. This combination may not have made the whale happy, but it probably did not poison him either. There is an interesting connection between the bumblebee and the monkshood plant (aconite). The bumblebee was frequently used as a magical charm by hunters. The monkshood is termed *anusnaadam ulanqin,* "the house of the bumblebee." The rationale is given by an Aleut, "Bumblebee goes in for a long time and later comes out." This is what the Aleuts wanted the spear to do in the whale. Thus, this magical transfer of like powers may explain their reason for including bumblebees in the magical poison. The elements of the poison were mixed until they stuck together and were then placed underneath the chipped stone point of the spear. The spear had a long whalebone receiver or head and with its wood shaft was only four feet (1.2 meters) in length. The chipped point was sometimes made of obsidian and was intended to break off inside when it hit bone. The spear was cast with a throwing board, thus assuring deep penetration.

Many or most of the whales struck by the whaler of one village were not recovered by his village but drifted onto another island and provided a kind of unearned increment. Since each village might receive a whale speared by some other village, there was, in effect, an "external economy."

SEA OTTER HUNTING

The most famous method of sea otter hunting employed a surround. Usually six kayaks or more went out together. They formed a generally straight line as they scanned an area. The man who sighted a sea otter immediately raised his paddle vertically above his head and remained stationary. The other five then formed a circle about him. If the sea otter dived again, the nearest man remained by it. Again, the others formed a circle. The animal seldom remained underwater more than six minutes, less on each successive dive. A light harpoon with a detachable ivory point was cast with the throwing board. The multibarbed point remained in the animal, but the harpoon floated back to serve as a drag. The point was attached to the harpoon shaft by a 15-foot (4.6 meters) sinew line in two places, first, on the lower wood shaft portion and second, near the juncture of the wood shaft and single-piece whalebone socket. These two attaching arms of the line formed a "Y," or martingale. Since the bone socket-piece was heavy, the harpoon floated vertically in the water with the fore-end down, thus serving as a drag on the sea otter and a marker for the pursuing hunter. Once the harpoon was set, the sea otter never escaped. Interestingly, the man whose harpoon point entered closest to the tail received ownership of the animal. Although one harpoon was sufficient, the hunters were in competition with each other and several men might cast at the same time.

Other harpoons had a bladder—a length of intestine or the stomach of a cormorant—attached parallel to the shaft. There were two major classes of harpoons defined by the spine or stiffness of the shaft. A stiff spine was used for a straight shot through the air. A more limber shaft was used for casting in the wind and for sliding on the water before entering the sea otter.

Another method of sea otter hunting took advantage of the fact that the sea otters haul up on rocky shores during severe storms. The hunters on one island would estimate when the storm would slacken on a remote island where sea otters were known to be. Then they would launch into the running surf in order to reach their destination while the storm was still strong enough to keep the sea otters on shore. Taking advantage of the screening noise of the wind and waves, they walked along the shore and clubbed the sea otters, sometimes with unusually rich results.

In pre-Russian times, the sea otter was an honored animal considered by the Aleuts to be of human origin. However, sea otter meat did not taste good and its skin was of limited value. Therefore, it was hunted infrequently until commercial hunting for furs was initiated by the Russians. The belief in the human origin of the sea otter did not prevent the Aleuts from hunting sea otters, although they observed many precautions to win the good will of the "person" of the sea otter. Always practical, the Aleuts were more interested in the edible than in the incredible.

With the arrival of the Russians and then the Americans, sea otter hunting became the preoccupation of the able-bodied Aleut men, whose superiority in skills for hunting sea otter was gained from early childhood training for kayak hunting. Europeans have never been able to acquire the necessary skills. They can learn to handle the kayak with fair skill in calm water, but they cannot hunt at the same time. The Aleuts had to hunt in foul weather. To launch a man in heavy surf, two hunters would pick up the kayak with the hunter already sealed in, drip skirt fastened, face and wrists tightly secured, and swing him into the waves from a rock shoulder.

Once safely clear of the reefs, the Aleut had to use a multitude of cues from the environment and only his memory to achieve his objective and to return home safely. He had to remember each turn he made and the length of each segment on a different bearing. Since he used wind direction as a cue, he had to note if the wind changed direction. To return, he then made the necessary course corrections, depending in large part on memory. Approaching an island, whether in fog or at night, he used the cues provided by shore birds, kelp beds, the sound of surf on rocks, currents, tidal flows, changes in water texture, and wave action. One hunter described his life as a sea otter hunter around the turn of the century and emphasized his feeling of abandonment. After leaving the deck of the small schooner, he saw the mast gradually disappear below the horizon and then he was alone.

One way to highlight the essential features of open sea kayak hunting is to note the major contrasts with land hunting. The sea is not an inert liquid that fills low spots in the earth's surface, nor is it a stable surface on which landlubbers can walk dependably. It is a living being. It is constantly shrugging its shoulders, flexing its muscles, heaving and rising, slacking and running, breaking into cliff-shattering waves or rarely and deceptively assuming a calm surface. The sea can quietly entice the hunter to a moment of forgetfulness, a moment that is sufficient to engulf and drown him. The land hunter never needs to worry that the surface he is traveling on will suddenly open up and swallow him. If he gets tired, he can lie down. There is no tidal schedule to observe. If caught in a snow storm in subzero weather, he can hole up and wait for the storm to pass. He dies by days and hours. The man who falls into cold water dies in minutes. Psychologically, the open sea hunter is living in a radically different world than the land hunter.

The Aleuts take pride in being Aleuts. Historically, one can see that they were proud of their marine adaptation, and in categories where comparisons could be made, such as kayak hunting, they knew that they were better than anyone else—whether Europeans, Eskimos, or Indians. The Russians were forced to depend upon Aleuts for sea-otter hunting; their monopoly was complete. They could not be duplicated nor replaced. As a consequence, Aleuts were taken to Sitka and to Fort Ross in California. Two Aleuts taken to Leningrad (then St. Petersburg) gave kayak demonstrations on the River Neva and enjoyed an appreciative audience. The daughter of the Unalaska Aleut who gave public exhibitions of kayaking in a pond at the St. Louis World's Fair glowed with pride as she described her father's experiences and the attention given him for his skill. Individually, the kayaking life reassured the Aleut that he was indeed a competent creature in a competitive arena where skill and knowledge, as well as physical endurance, were the prerequisites for survival and where each man literally sank or swam on his own individual merits.

OTHER FORMS OF HUNTING AND COLLECTING

Other forms of hunting were equally important to the dietary intake of the Aleuts, although they were less dramatic and technologically more simple. Collecting eggs required agility for climbing on cliffs, and catching ducks with a bolas required a good sense of timing. These skills were less demanding, however, and were within the capabilities of women. Octopus, certainly a major dietary item, were simply drawn from their submarine caves and crevices with gaffs and, since they were seldom more than six (1.8 meters) or eight feet (2.4 meters) in diameter, the hunter could walk back to shore swaddled in tentacles, with no possible chance of losing his game.

There was a simplicity of technology that resulted from Aleut ingenuity and knowledge of animal habits. The snare for catching puffins consists only of a light wood stake some 18 inches long (0.46 meter) and a noose of sinew line or, in later times, only a piece of hard lay halibut line. Tufted puffins were sought particularly for their skins, which made excellent parkas. The skins were, naturally, better without spear holes in them. In the evening, after the puffins had fallen asleep, the Aleuts climbed up to the nesting area and placed the snare in the ground in front of an entry hole. The noose was smeared with mud to conceal it and to make it conform to the hole. The following morning the puffin ran out of its little cave as usual, spread its short wings for the rapid descent to the ocean below, and announced its presence with an ungraceful choking sound. In so doing, it automatically hanged itself in the noose. Aleuts collected puffins, skinned them out over the beak in one piece, ate the meat, and turned the skins over to the women for preparation.

In each case, for any bird, mammal, or fish, there were alternate methods of catching the prey. Sometimes the wing bone of a puffin was fastened crosswise on a stick and the Aleut inserted this into the puffin cave and wound the bird up on the device. Nets were also used.

Earlier we noted two relevant points. There are many ecological niches or habitats to be exploited and many of these can be simultaneously exploited by different cohorts of the population. Table 4.1 shows the habitats keyed to the kinds of individuals who can exploit them. The general arrangement reflects mobility. But mobility is not uniformly equated with the amount of edible food returned to the village. A major strength of the Aleut population system lies in the fact that old people and young children make a significant contribution to the total food intake of the village. The terrestrial requirements of an Aleut village can be defined as the distance a little old woman can walk between sunrise and sunset and collect roots or basketry grass. A six-mile (10 kilometers) radius would be a conservative estimate. The enormous layers of sea urchin shell in the village middens throughout the Aleutian chain testify to the significant contribution of women, children, and old persons.

Table 4.2 presents an estimate of the relative contribution of the different kinds of foods. Any one of these categories could vary by 5 to 10 percent in successive years, in the same village and between villages, and in different parts of the chain. Table 4.3 shows the more specific uses of different parts of the Stellar sea lion.

Hunger, but not starvation, might occur in March, but whole villages never become extinct as a consequence of starvation alone. The environmental biomass that surrounds the Aleuts is large and stable, and the Aleuts have techniques for exploiting every part of their world.

TABLE 4.1.   HABITATS KEYED TO KINDS OF INDIVIDUALS

Individuals	Inland	Lakes & Streams	Beach	Reef	Bay	Offshore Islands	Cliffs	Open Sea
Old infirm females	+	+	+	+	+	−	−	−
Old infirm males	−	+	+	+	+	−	−	−
Pregnant women	(+)	−	(+)	(+)	(+)	−	−	−
Children	+	+	+	+	+	(+)	(+)	−
Young to middle-aged females	−	(+)	+	+	+	+	+	−
Young to middle-aged males	(+)	+	+	+	+	+	+	+

(Increasing mobility from top to bottom)

Beginning with the kinds of people, their use of the habitats is indicated by a plus sign. Parentheses indicate qualified use or special limitations. This chart provides no indication of the different methods of using the same area nor the different resources procured. Thus old men hand-line fish the bay from boats; old women fish from the shore. Men collect driftwood suitable for manufacture of boat frames; women collect driftwood suitable only for fuel.

Fig. 14a. Amchitka, 1968. Sea otters in a typical posture for sleeping, eating, or waving to humans.

Fig. 14b. Amchitka, 1968. Two large bull sea lions with cows on right.

Fig. 14c. Nikolski, 1970. Mrs. Eva Chercasen scraping a sea lion stomach and preparing it for use as a container for storing salmon.

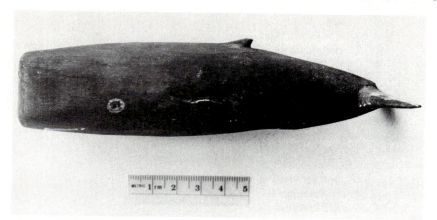

Fig. 14d. Colored carved wood model of sperm whale. Made on the island of Unalaska in 1817 for Chamisso. Each family of whales is represented by a model carved from a single piece of wood. One of the Aleut names collected by Chamisso is an Attu name; the others were given in the Fox Island dialect. The original pigments have endured, with the aid of good scientific conservation (photo by Bruno Frøhlich, 1978, for Museum für Naturkunde, Berlin).

Fig. 14e. Nikolski, 1973. Mr. George Bezezekoff of Nikolski holding two halibut, one showing upper side and the other showing the lower side.

Fig. 14f. Nikolski, 1952. Pogies (greenlings) netted on the Nikolski reef. The dip net and gaff are often used together; the gaff alone is used for octopus.

Fig. 14g. Nikolski, 1952. Mrs. Eva Chercasen weaving a grass basket with open
mesh for draining, intended for collecting
sea urchins, mussels, chitons, and other
invertebrates from the reef. Most baskets
are woven upside down, sometimes with
a suspension device.

Fig. 14h. Tufted puffin sunning himself.

Fig. 14i. Cormorants, one sitting and one
in flight.

TABLE 4.2

Type of Food	Percentage of Total Diet
Marine mammals	30
Fishes	30
Birds and eggs	20
Invertebrates	15
Plants	Less than 5

TABLE 4.3.   MULTIPLE USE OF NORTHERN OR STELLER SEA LION

Part of Animal	Partial List of Uses
1. Hide	Cover for kayak and umiak; line for harpoon
2. Flesh	Food, for humans
3. Blubber	Food: eaten with meat, rendered for oil
4. Organs (heart, liver, spleen, kidney)	Food
5. Bones	Ribs for root diggers; humerus for club; baculum for flaker
6. Teeth	Decorative pendants; fishhooks
7. Whiskers	Decoration of wood hunting hats and visors
8. Sinew	Back sinews using for sewing, lashing, cordage (less desirable than sinew of whale or caribou)
9. Flippers	Soles used for boot soles; contents gelatinized in flipper and eaten
10. Pericardium	Water bottle, general-purpose container
11. Esophagus	Parka, pants, leggings of boots, pouches
12. Stomach	Storage container (especially for dried salmon) (see Fig. 14c)
13. Intestines	Parka, pants, pouches

5/Ancient village life

A seventeenth-century visitor to an Aleut village would most likely have been delighted in the picturesque setting, kayaks plying the waters in front of the village, perhaps an umiak-load of people returning from an egg-collecting expedition, and a wheeling, screaming cluster of gulls stealing scraps of fish entrails from the stream or beach where women were cleaning them. He might have seen rack after rack of drying salmon but he might well have overlooked the houses themselves and wondered where the people lived.

HOUSES AND HOUSEHOLDS

An entire village of 200 or more Aleuts could be contained in no more than five houses. Such houses were accordingly very large. Being semisubterranean, covered with growing grass and entered through hatchways in the roof, they blended with the green hills and were not immediately distinguishable. The early Russian hunters sometimes referred to them as caves and took advantage of the fact that the Aleuts could emerge only one at a time from each hatch, to kill them, one at a time. Such underground houses have been variously called *yurts* and *barabaras*. These two terms are Russian and the latter is specifically a Siberian term sometimes converted to *barrabkie*. They were warm, capacious, and admirably suited for this wet and windy environment.

The size varied so greatly that one cannot give typical dimensions without many qualifications, but they all had in common the fact that they were rectangular rather than square. Before the Russians and during the early years of their occupation, a *barabara* was made by first digging an area some 12 to 20 meters in length, 6 to 10 meters in width, and 1.5 to 2 meters in depth. This house excavation often went through older houses, sometimes the very old stone-based houses, burials, and occupational debris. The Unalaska Aleuts told Veniaminov that some villages had *barabaras* more than 85 meters in length. Solovioff gives a length of 73 meters for a house in the same district and I have measured one such house pit near Nikolski as approximately 55 meters in length. However, the majority of houses were certainly smaller, and the smaller villages had only small houses. Houses 6 meters by 12 meters appear frequently in the surface depressions of abandoned villages. There has also been a trend, beginning before 1800 A.D., toward smaller houses with a door in the end, culminating in wood frame houses for individual families found in the villages today. The more traditional *barabaras*, with an entryway chamber (*kalador*) and end door, still survive in the summer camps (Fig. 15).

The construction required large numbers of split timbers, many adze-hewn planks, sod, and grass. Whalebone, ribs, and mandible bones often supplemented the timbers as roof beams and rafters. Vertical posts were set for the walls and longer posts were placed inside these, toward the interior, to carry cross beams which, in turn, supported the rafters. Short pieces were run between the rafters and a thatching of long grass lay directly upon them. Usually, but subject to variation, earth was placed on the grass, and turf or sod was then added. The latter continued to grow and blend into the surrounding grass. The introduction of cows and goats by the Russians was viewed in rather a dim light (windows were introduced later), for they sometimes grazed over a house and fell through the roof. The Aleuts did not totally disapprove of the Russian interest in livestock; they were, however, concerned about the overhead.

Hatches were built into the center of the roof and served for light, as outlets for smoke, and for entry and exit. Ladders consisted of notched logs that permitted only one person at a time to enter or leave. For a festival, the ladder might be replaced with a line of inflated bladders, a sure test of dignity as well as of dex-

Fig. 15. Gerald Berreman and Philip Spaulding emerging from an underground barabara *at Sand Beach, near Nikolski, Umnak Island, 1952.*

terity for the arriving guests. There were few firehearths as such, and pit cooking was usually done outside the house. Lamps were used and they gave off enough heat to permit people to lie about in comfort.

Lamps could produce soot and smoke in significant quantities. An old lady once told me that the oil of the killer whale or sperm whale burned best in lamps, for it left the babies' faces clean in the morning. Lamp oil from baleen whales and from seals created more soot and the babies' faces had to be wiped off in the morning. Such carbon has been identified in the lungs of an eighteenth-century mummy from the Kagamil burial caves (Zimmerman, 1971).

Women tended the lamps, though a man might do so, if necessary. In this case, he was careful to use sticks to move the moss wick and he carefully avoided direct contact with the sea mammal oil. Women owned the lamps, though they were made by men. This is probably related to their ownership of houses or of cubicles within the larger houses. In addition to the lamps, the women owned all the furniture, the lamp stands, matting, basketry, wood dishes and box containers, sewing equipment (awls, knobbed needles, eyed needles, scrapers, abraders, root diggers), but not the children's cradles. These were owned by the children. A man might sleep in a cradle, which had then to be made larger for him, and he might be buried (after suitable preparation) in his cradle.

Each family consisted of grandparents, parents, and their children, sometimes including a niece or nephew of the mother. All lived in cubicles or compartments around the sides and back end of the house. The most honored position was always at the far back. The compartments were well separated by posts and suspended woven grass mats. A daughter who was in the process of being married and was being visited by her suitor had her own cubicle. Most or all of the families in a house were related to each other and one headman presided over this household of relatives. Each house had a headman, and thus a village could have as many headmen as there were households. The headman also presided over a hunting unit composed of the able-bodied males of the household, both for *baidarka* hunting and also for hunting, fishing, or traveling, and using the *baidar* (umiak). Secret compartments might be dug out in the sides of the *barabara* and concealed behind the wall mats. Children were concealed in these compartments during raids. There appears to be an important correspondence between the headman of a large household and the composition of the household. His prestige and effectiveness as a leader was dependent in part upon the number of relatives whom he housed and organized in their hunting, fishing, and collecting activities. Even a very old headman who could no longer organize and participate in hunting retained an honored position in the back of the house.

A seventeenth-century visitor would also have seen the image of the deity. This figurine was suspended from a ceiling beam where the hunter could speak with him before going out and report on his return. Whether each male family head owned such an image or whether there was only one for each house cannot be accurately inferred from the excavations of such figures, the published sources, or from the few Aleuts themselves who are still familiar with the images. The houses of 4000 years ago were smaller than those of 1000 years ago and the few numbers of the suspended form of the image of the deity that have been identified may correspond to the numbers of houses. Clerical sources understandably have little to say about the original Aleut religious beliefs and practices.

Large villages shrank in the summer and small villages swelled in size. In order to make the best possible use of the various salmon streams and to collect special foods, birds, and roots that are more common in some localities, the people usually made a summer excursion, breaking into smaller family units and reoccupying unused houses or setting up tents in a variety of summer villages. This summer dispersal was not only economically important, it also provided a release from cabin fever and permitted people to resort themselves into compatible groups for the summer activities of gathering berries, eggs, salmon, and roots.

DANCING, SINGING, AND WRESTLING

Visits between villages were a major social event. Many of the guests arrived in *baidars* as well as in *baidarkas* and all were dressed in their best clothes. For the men, this meant the elaborate conical wood hat with much decoration. The dances were staged inside a large *barabara*. There were several kinds of dances, involving both men and women. There might be several drummers, using different sizes of circular tambourine drums. Individuals could rise and offer a song, and occasionally there was song dueling. A man might sing a song that was slightly derisive, at least by implication, of another man. The recipient in turn might offer a similar song. Wrestling was also a form of contest between members of different villages. When the entertainment took the form of wrestling, the host villagers might tilt the outcome by planting sharp pointed knives in the dance floor. These bifacially chipped points were some 20 centimeters in length. The base was fixed firmly in the packed earth floor and then they were covered with grass. The grass that always covered the floor was pushed back for the dances and, therefore, these knives could escape notice. The visiting opponent was thrown upon such a knife when the opportunity presented itself. Wrestlers used charms and amulets, including grease from a mummy or "a piece of dead man," but the impaling knife was more effective.

The stomach of a seal was used in at least one dance form. A similar dance has been portrayed by an eighteenth-century artist in which bladders are carried (around 1775; Fedorova, 1973). A male dancer holding two stomachs is portrayed in an ivory carving contained in the superb Aleut collections in the National Museum of Finland in Helsinki. An interesting variation in this dance, which has gone unnoticed, is that the position of the stomach could be used as a signal for an attack on the visitors. The hair seal stomach was ordinarily carried by a man with the pyloric end (the aperture leading to the intestines) facing the dancer. When the man turned the pyloris outward, facing the visitors, the attack began. It should be emphasized that fighting between villages was comparatively rare, though not unknown, and that the song dueling, wrestling, and other forms of public contest functioned to settle feuds and to resolve bad feelings, while the dancing and gift-giving created good will. Headmen were responsible for the lodging and feeding of visitors, and, as always, for seeing that they enjoyed their visit.

INSPECTION AND SCANNING SYSTEM

Each village maintained a formal and informal inspection and scanning system that was prepared to inform the inhabitants of anything noteworthy on sea, land, and air for a long distance, 8 kilometers or more in certain directions. It was possible for the people at Chaluka to see boats setting out from the village on Anangula, about 8 kilometers northwest. The people on Anangula could see boats entering and leaving the village in Okee Bay some 5 kilometers to their northeast. Continuing on around Umnak Island with its 27 villages, communication between villages was fairly simple. Since people in contiguous villages were closely related to each other, this constant sea inspection system was a valuable means of extracting the maximum possible amounts of mammals and driftwood from the sea. Whether it was possible for a whale or sea lion to circle Umnak Island without being intercepted is an interesting question. As the population size increased, and the number of villages also grew, it was necessary for the Aleuts to observe various rules of good behavior, such as avoiding hunting or fishing in front or another village. At the same time, this distribution of villages made it possible for a lagging traveler to find accommodations and entertainment for the night instead of having to camp alone. Hospitality was a prominent feature of Aleut life and there were frequent visitors from different villages. They often had a relative or a "best friend" to whom they went for food and lodging, and reciprocally, they hosted the same person.

WARFARE

Warfare between villages was most often between those in different dialect groups, or with the Koniag Eskimos of the Alaska Peninsula beyond Port Moller on the north side and Kupreanof Point on the south side. Much more commonly, villages aided each other, reciprocating with festivals in which dancing, singing, games, and gifts were important. The villages were linked together by genealogy bonds and common dialect.

Warfare most often consisted of raiding and seldom involved large numbers of persons. The Atka Aleuts sometimes raided as far as Umnak and one "war" took place after the chapel had been established at Chaluka, sometime between 1795 and 1800. In this event the Aleuts living at Natokagh (now called Sandy Beach), a one-hour walk south of Chaluka, first saw the invading Atka *baidarkas* and fired the one muzzle-loader permitted them by the Russians for signaling. One young nursing mother in front of the chapel on Chaluka was surprised as the Chaluka men repulsed the Atka men with harpoons. The fact that she was nursing her baby and could not run is given as much prominence as the fighting. Only seven Atka men participated in this war, and one of them stayed by the *baidarkas* to keep them ready for the scheduled strategic retreat.

A review of Aleut stories indicates that these forays were usually raids, carefully planned but of limited objective, most often intended to satisfy an insult or to maintain a feud. The most portable property of real value were females and these were usually obtained in a less hazardous fashion. Taking children for slaves apparently occurred primarily in the eastern Aleutians and in limited form. A careful study of a few hundred skeletons has revealed little in the way of knife marks or other wounds. The knife marks on skeletons of the Medvedev party are clear evidence of lethal hostilities. Rod armor, a vest made of small vertical rods of wood held together with sinew, was recovered from the warm cave on Kagamil, and a tradition persists that only a headman was entitled to wear such armor.

CLOTHING

Aleuts wore very colorful clothing. The man's conical wooden hat with paintings and ivory figures on it, the woman's sea-otter parka, and the three-piece boots were technical achievements that have drawn high praise. They required much time, many materials, and automatically account for a large proportion of the women's working hours and a lesser portion of the men's. It would have been impossible to walk through a village for even a few hours without seeing a woman making or repairing clothing.

The best thread was sinew taken from the back and tail of a whale and from caribou. Kept in chunks or billets of a cubit or so in length, a single fiber, smaller than our number 50 thread, was teased out and inserted into the eye of a very small bone needle. This lead fiber served to draw out a larger thread of several fibers twisted into a tough thread. With this, the thin strips of intestine could be sewn together into the horizontally banded *kamleika* or waterproof parka with a drawstring about the hood. The toughest material was the flipper of the sea lion, used for boot soles. These water boots were light, warm, and waterproof, and survived along with the *kamleikas* long after the birdskin and fur clothing was abandoned. The upper of the boot was made of hair seal with the hair removed, and the leggings that extended above the knees were made of esophagus, most often the gullet of the hair seal or sea lion (Fig. 16). Many of these seams sewn over the folded edge of the two pieces joined together and were, therefore, quite watertight. Whale sinew characteristically swells a little when wet, thereby plugging the needle hole even more tightly. Women also gathered and dried the grass used in place of socks. This grass could be easily replaced when too worn and was always available for use as tinder on trips when a campfire was built or a lamp was lit. Woven grass socks were also made but these were not common and were worn only inside the house.

For themselves, they made a hoodless parka of sea otter skins with a standing collar. These were called *suk* and were also made of intestines and of bird skins. The sea otter parkas are found in the mummy caves but they rapidly went out of use because of the Russian demand for sea otter skins. The men more often wore birdskin parkas, without hoods—far and away the most common garment. Boots were not worn and were often carried, rather than worn, to save wear and tear, especially when walking over snow. Pants were worn even less often. They employed a drawstring similar to that of the *kamleika*. Some, if not all, were made in emulation of Russian trousers.

The skins of about 40 tufted puffins or 25 cormorants made one full-length

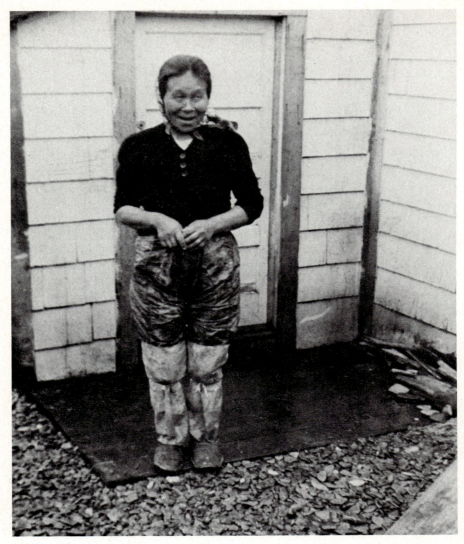

Fig. 16. Mrs. Eva Chercasen of Nikolski wears seal esophagus pants and boots of seal esophagus and uppers and sea lion flipper soles.

parka. These were often reversible, though the feathers were usually worn on the inside in cold weather. In warm weather and on social occasions the feathers were worn on the outside. Such a parka could be worn a full year or more. The waterproof *kamleika*, in contrast, wore out more quickly, since it was made of intestines of the sea lion or of the brown bear if made by an Aleut woman on Unimak Island or on the Alaska Peninsula. Sometimes *kamleikas* were made of esophagus of seal or sea lion, or the tongue skin of a whale. Instead of a standing collar, the *kamleika* had a hood with drawstring, and the wrists were tied for sea travel. The garment also reached below the knees.

The length of these garments made it practical for the wearer to squat over a small lamp for warmth, and hunters often carried a small lamp to be used in this way. Some late-style lamps even had an eye or a knob so that they could be attached to a belt. *Kamleikas,* worn only by men, were beautifully decorated. At the hem, sections of red, green, brown, or black alternated, and sewn between the rows of intestine were white rump feathers from the cormorant, or white feathers from the common bald eagle. Small pieces of colored esophagus might also be inserted in the seams. The same technology that was used in making the clothing was used in manufacturing pouches and bags which were made well into the 1960s.

The crowning glory of the well-dressed man was a magnificent wooden hat (Fig. 17). These lavishly embellished hats gave some indication of wealth and competence. They were always worn by important men, especially for festivals and visits between villages. They were made of wood, carefully scraped thin and sanded, then steamed to form an asymmetrical cone, with the long side in front projecting well over the eyes of the man. It was considered good form to conceal the eyes in approaching unidentified people or those whose intentions might be dubious, just as it was impolite for a young person to look directly into the face of an older person. The seam was placed at the back of the head and concealed with a bone plate that ran vertically to the top and was secured with sinew or baleen.

A more common type of wooden headgear was the visor or hat with open top. Although also painted and festooned with sea lion whiskers, and perhaps a little seated figure of a man in front—possibly an image of the deity—the projecting decorations were confined to one side. This was because the throwing arm passed close to the side of the head in swinging the throwing board or in casting a larger sea lion or a porpoise harpoon.

LABRETS AND TATTOOS

The faces and hands were tattooed, bone or ivory pins were thrust through the septum of the nose, and sea otter teeth or other bangles might depend from such a septal pin. Ivory ear plugs were set in the ear lobes, or feathers (seen in the mummies), and a pair of labrets were commonly worn in the lower lip at the corners of the mouth. These labrets took many forms and a single large one might be centrally placed. All had in common an enlarged base or flange—not unlike the brim of a hat—that prevented the labret from falling out. They have varied over 4000 years as seen in Chaluka. The earliest ones were usually ivory and were thin. The latest ones, seen in the Kagamil caves and with seventeenth- and eighteenth-century burials, were more often fatter. Frequently the exposed portion was round. They were made of ivory, whalebone, the dense bone of the whale ear, stone, lignite, and wood. The lower lip of the infant was pierced within the first year of life. A small plug was inserted from the inside and this was later replaced with a larger one.

All in all, the ancient Aleuts made a distinguished and colorful appearance. The polychrome paintings of the man's hat, the colored tabs, feather inserts of his *kamleika,* a muscular brown face, and small powerful hands proclaimed the presence of a capable person. The women were equally distinguished with their

ДЕРЕВЯННЫЕ ОХОТНИЧЬИ ШЛЯПЫ-
ЧАСТЬ ПРОМЫСЛОВОГО СНАРЯЖЕНИЯ ОХОТНИКА.
ВЫТЯНУТЫЙ КОЗЫРЕК ЗАЩИЩАЕТ ГЛАЗА ОТ БЛЕСКА СОЛНЦА.
БОГАТО УКРАШЕННЫЕ ШЛЯПЫ ИМЕЛИСЬ ТОЛЬКО У РОДОВОЙ ЗНАТИ,
ТАК КАК БЫЛИ ОЧЕНЬ ДОРОГИ.
ОДИН ГОЛОВНОЙ УБОР ПО ЦЕНЕ БЫЛ РАВЕН БАЙДАРКЕ ИЛИ ДВУМ-ТРЕМ РАБАМ.

Fig. 17. Ceremonial hats, which are worn only by males during visits and ceremonies.

jet black hair gathered in a bun, their incomparably smooth complexions, reflecting a roseate brown that contrasted subtly with their luxurious sea otter fur garments. A visitor would be equally impressed with the smooth features of the children and their very large heads, long trunks, and the disciplined energy of their quick movements. Whether sitting on their haunches with legs stretched in front, squatting on the ground, or standing in a kayak and riding it into the beach, the Aleuts presented a dignified appearance.

PATTERNS FOR LIVING

The architects of Aleutian culture designed a series of patterns for living that provided law without lawyers and leaders without elections. The codes for conduct were drilled into each individual. Like Swiss watches, each Aleut had his own mainspring. With proper oiling, occasional resetting, and daily winding, he performed as his cultural preceptors had designed him to perform.

As mentioned earlier, the major concern of the village community was the maintenance of the peace. Little attention was given to punishment of offenders, for this did little to restore the peace. The rare person who was incorrigible, who repeatedly stole things or women, might be put to death after a general consultation among the village elders. Two criteria—whether the offense was genuinely a threat to the peace of the community and whether it was done repeatedly or there was adequate evidence that the offender would again repeat his indiscretion—were guides for village elders to make this decision.

The headmen, called chiefs by Americans, were heads of households and thus spoke for many relatives. They had no anointed power in the sense of the divine right of kings, nor any hereditary power that automatically passed from father to son. They were successful hunters, physically strong, and capable of good judgment. They could give good advice on matters connected with hunting and movement of the village from winter quarters to the summer camps, and they could suggest that a child be adopted or that a lookout be posted where he could alert the village to the presence of whales or enemies.

Another kind of leader who might be a different person from the headman was the "strong man." He was, as his name implies, a physically strong person but he was known and named for this endowment. He could lift stones or boats with men in them, carry half a sea lion in one hand without getting blood on his parka, or kill three men at one time by strangling one in each hand and a third between his legs. Such men underwent special training, were properly famed, but then died prematurely.

Each person was bound to many others in a web of relationships which provided him with tutors, friends, hunting partners, and younger persons who would tend him in old age. The names given a child helped to establish him. Even the spirit of a deceased person could be transferred with his name. In another kind of relationship, two people (usually an adult and a newborn or a child) were made *anaaqisagh* to each other—that is, they were dependent upon each other. A woman who was appointed *anaaqisagh* to a young child by its parents had then to make sure that the child received adequate food, clothing, and opportunities for play and instruction. If the child were criticized, the older person was automatically criticized at the same time and came to the defense of the child. If an indiscreet visitor to a house complained that an infant cried too much, its *anaaqisagh* might cry to place herself in the same position and thus share a portion of the criticism. On the other hand, the older person might also pick up a club (made of yellow cedar or of bone) and whack the critic over the head. The relationship was well composed, for as the older person aged and needed help, the younger member of the chronologically tandem pair felt a natural desire to provide whatever help was indicated. The older individual helped the younger person into the world and the younger one helped the older person on the way out.

If two persons shared the same name, they were believed to have the basis for sympathetic behavior, or if they had a similar appearance or had the same accident befall them, they were "like each other" and might use this similarity as a common bond for friendship and for sharing food or other supplies.

KINSHIP TERMS

Genealogical reckoning was intricate, far more complex than among Europeans, and is shown in the number of kinship terms—about 56—and the distinctions they entailed. Among the categories of distinctions made were those between the different kinds of cousins. Your father's brother's son was a relative whom you "may have for a brother," and therefore could not marry, even if you were a female of appropriate age. The son or daughter of your mother's brother or of your father's sister was not automatically prohibited. In actual practice, wives were usually secured from a different household and more often from a different village. The father of a young man usually kept an eye out for a suitable wife for his son and might initiate the arrangements for getting her home to his village. At least for villages within easy traveling distance and within the same dialectical area, the young man often went to serve his prospective parents-in-law, remaining there until the first child was born.

Not only were aunts and uncles of the mother and father distinguished from each other, but nieces and nephews were as well, with sex-distinguishing terms used for both. Still another system of organization accompanied this pigeon-holing—the relative age of the person involved if they were in the same category. Thus "older" or "younger brother" and "older" or "younger sister" were termed differently.

STORY TELLING

Story telling was one of the great arts of the Aleuts, from Port Moller to Attu. Stories were told most often in the evening when the younger people were in bed. The story was told beginning in a loud voice, and pursued with vigor and authority. Some were long, running on for two or more hours. Others were short and took no more than a few minutes. There were legendary stories that told of the origins of humans and animals. There were accounts of intrepid men who had traveled through storms, slain many Koniag Eskimos, and used their personal magic to great advantage. There were little stories that men composed while kayaking, perhaps an account of what a partner did on a hunting trip. In some places, as on Umnak, the women had different stories from the men, ones that they usually told. All stories were rendered in elocutionary fashion and compelled attention.

One style, described by Mr. William Tcheriapanoff of Akutan, involved frequent pauses by the speaker followed by an approving prolonged "mmmmmmmmm" by the listeners. If you came up to a tent at night, it sounded strange to hear the orator pronounce with vigor and the antiphony of approval from the congregation. It was important not to be bashful. One point of this form of audience participation was the approval of accuracy and style. When stories were told in the dark, it was probably the only way the orator had of knowing whether his audience was awake. A man was never corrected when he made a mistake. When a man told a story over again, or came to a section with some repetition where he could rectify his error, a listener might then tell him that "it is better, better hold it that way." This same system of rewarding persons for good behavior rather than criticizing them for mistakes extended to all things, whether in the manufacture of kayaks or in casting a harpoon. Even if the listeners laughed when the teller made a mistake, it was still considered impolite to tell him that he had made a mistake. Evening story telling was the appropriate way of ending the day. All persons looked forward to hearing or telling a story.

The crowning achievement of Aleut society was silence, whenever it was necessary to maintain privacy and individual equilibrium. Aleuts followed two rules in this respect: (1) if they had nothing worthwhile to say about someone or something they said nothing; and, (2) if they had nothing to say, they said nothing. Old men sat on the roofs over their houses by the hour and by the day, scanning the sea and sky, sometimes returning to their bed at night without a word to anyone. Life in a large house with 30 or 40 people would have been impossible without careful inculcation in rules for behavior. If a person could not have withdrawn from interaction, no matter how friendly, he would have been exhausted.

The habit of careful observation enabled people to determine from another's face some idea of whether he would be disturbed by an intrusion through his eardrums. The correlative habits of not touching each other unnecessarily—such as by handshaking and backslapping—and of showing deference to each person based upon friendship, kinship, age, sex, and prestige made for a harmonious and cohesive group. Add to this the intensive training in endurance and self-sufficiency and the result is the Aleut village, a cooperative unit that could strain the bay of all necessary foods during the day and stage a festival the same evening, disbursing the gains of the hunt to everyone in the village and their guests.

6/The whale swimming north: Anangula

Looking northwest from Nikolski, the horizon of the Bering Sea is interrupted by the profile of an island that looks like a whale swimming north. This is the way the ancient Aleuts viewed this island. The blunt head of the island is named with a word that means "bust" or "head" of a sea mammal (*qiiganga*). The low-lying southern tail of the island is named with a word that can be used either for the tail of a fish or of a whale (*chmagh*). Therefore, the combination of the names for the head and tail of the island indicate that it was conceived as a whale. The indentation of a shallow valley behind the head, where there was a small village, is named the "neck." The name of the island, Anangula, is an older Aleut form whose meaning is lost in antiquity. The current name used on sailing charts, Ananiuliak, is an anglicized variation of a recent form of the name. Since the introduction of Belgian hares around 1936, the island has also been known locally as Rabbit Island (Fig. 18).

The island is fringed by a broad wave-cut terrace, some seven meters in height, and steep cliffs rise from the wave-washed terrace in many places. Gulls dominate the bird life, attacking eagles and ravens with vigor and occasionally snatching a rabbit as well. In 1974, five Soviet scientists and seven Americans, including one Aleut, Mrs. O. Krukoff of Nikolski, witnessed a gull swallow a rabbit, and then spend two or three days digesting its victim. The bird seized the rabbit near the brow of a cliff, carried it down to the marine terrace 50 feet (15.25 meters) below, and swallowed it slowly, head first. Eagles, peregrine hawks, ravens, eider ducks, tufted puffins, horned puffins, least auklets, whiskered auklets, cormorants, shearwaters, murres, finches, and other dickeybirds decorate the cliffs and patrol the waters according to their individual habits.

Sea lions and harbor seals occasionally swim about the island, usually clockwise, and infrequently, an insouciant sea otter or a humpback whale passes by. Deep rye grass cloaks the upper reaches of the terrace and low-lying portions of the island, giving way to alpine heather balds ascending the island to its 90-meter hump. The most spectacular blaze of flowers is the dense stand of aconite (*Aconitum maximum*) which turns into a deep blue in August, covering an entire abandoned village site and providing homes for large bumblebees.

In 1938, I was walking over the tail end of the island with Mr. Alan G. May, a veteran of three years with Dr. Aleš Hrdlička, and saw, glistening in the light mist that shrouded the area, several hundred stone tools lying exposed in blowouts. None

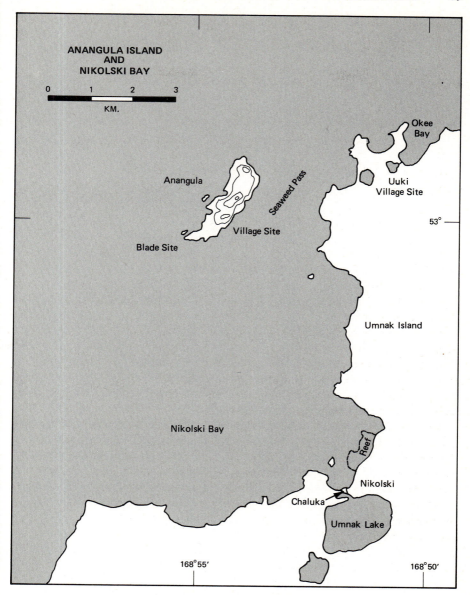

Fig. 18. Anangula Island and Nikolski Bay.

of the tools looked like very much. There was very little flaking on them, and what flaking existed was on only one surface. They seemed crude in comparison with the finely flaked knives and points of later Aleut culture with which we were familiar. Nevertheless, they were tools, some pointed, and they included a few cores from which prismatic blades had been struck. We made small collections and reported them to Dr. Hrdlička, who decided that probably a sample of "the better ones" should be sent back to the Smithsonian, but that we could keep the others. It was fortunate that we kept a sample because many years later they provided the clue to the oldest Aleut occupation and led directly to the unraveling of the origin of the Aleuts and to the discovery of the first known permanent village in the Aleutian Islands.

Following the advice and encouragement of the late Dr. Louis J. Giddings, a genuinely great and productive arctic archeologist with whom I discussed these cores and unifacial blades, I returned to Anangula in 1952. With Mr. Afenogin K. Ermeloff as our preceptor, a large part of the population of Nikolski took us out to the island, a 40-minute trip in the old dories. We spent the day collecting eider and gull eggs, catching rabbits for pets for the children, gathering grass for baskets, and enjoying familiar sights and the delightful bouquet of fragrances from flowers and the sea. Our beachcombing finds included Japanese glass fishing net floats thrown high with driftwood in the winter storms. Baby birds were sought after for pets but only the young gulls and eider ducks were caught.

Our *palatka*, a low-walled canvas tent with buttons to close the front opening that had been handmade from an old Russian model, was placed on the terrace at the foot of the steep incline below the Anangula village site. The Aleut name for this place was "the landing of Anangula village." In the morning, we were awakened by the puffins, shuttling down from their dens in the brows of the cliffs to the ocean where they splashed in. With their short, stubby wings, the puffins are awkward in taking off and poor in flying and landing. Their raspy voices decline as they descend. They always appear to be confused in their directions, seldom staying on one course more than a minute or two. The Aleut word of caution, "Never follow a puffin," is good advice. Another bird that woke us up was a least auklet, with its distinctive call, "kdii, kdii." We were told that in Akutan the same birds says "knii," and the people there know it is time to get up.

Like the Aleuts before us, we caught puffins with snares placed at the mouths of their dens after they had gone to sleep in the evening. In the morning, they strangled themselves on their take-off run. They were skinned inside out so that the skins could be used for parkas, and we relished their meat. A harbor seal provided excellent liver, fried in its blubber, and enough meat for us and for gifts to the village when we returned. Mr. Ermeloff shot the seal on the far side of the island on a little offshore rock, and pulled him back to shore with a retrieving hook. Lacking backpacks, he divided the meat into three portions, each wrapped in long green grass bundles with the skin in a separate bundle. Aleuts usually carried a stout line with a wood handle at one end, and also a retrieving hook on a longer line five or six fathoms in length. The lines passed over our shoulders in front and supported the bundles on our backs. We packed the seal back to our *palatka* in the same way that Aleuts had probably carried the same kinds of loads 9000 years earlier.

THE PLACE FOR MAKING STONE BLADES

In 1962, we secured some charcoal specimens for radiocarbon dating by following the tools exposed on the surface, down an inclined surface to the larger culture zone that was buried under two to three meters of volcanic ash and old soils. Christy G. Turner made another observation at the same time. Not only did these ancient Aleuts walk out to the Anangula Blade Site when Anangula Island was a part of Umnak Island, but they might have walked out to Umnak Island from further east when lower sea levels made Umnak the end of the Bering Land Bridge —the same way lemmings reached Umnak.

The radiocarbon dates were exciting because they showed that Aleut people had lived here at least 765 years, between 7660 and 8425 years ago. These dates were verified and augmented by the analysis of a total of 33 radiocarbon dates, which showed that the people had lived here for about 1500 years, between 7200 and 8700 years ago (see Table 6.1). The large number of firehearth specimens indicates many houses or cubicles within houses, although the outlines of the houses themselves are obscure.

The stone tools from the Blade Site do not look like much at first glance. However, these tools show connections with Asia, and they prove that the earliest Aleuts entered this area with a well-developed culture. They show that the ma-

TABLE 6.1

Specimen	Date (years ago)			Specimen	Date (years ago)	
	Libby Half-Life (5570 Years)	Penn Half-Life (5740 Years)			Libby Half-Life (5570 Years)	Penn Half-Life (5740 Years)
0. GX 2232	6600 ± 320	6798 ± 330		23. P 1104	8129 ± 96	8373 ± 99
				24. SI-2182	8140 ± 485	8384 ± 500
	Hiatus (ash III)			25. GX 2240	8170 ± 240	8415 ± 247
1. P 1836	6992 ± 91	7202 ± 93		26. P 1103	8173 ± 87	8418 ± 90
2. P 1835	7000 ± 91	7210 ± 93		27. SI-2179	8235 ± 125	8482 ± 129
3. GX 2233	7070 ± 240	7282 ± 247		28. GX 2239	8280 ± 220	8528 ± 227
4. GX 2235	7120 ± 240	7334 ± 247		29. GX 2231	8290 ± 240	8539 ± 247
5. GX 2241	7175 ± 240	7390 ± 247		30. SI-2176	8390 ± 95	8642 ± 98
6. GX 2237	7180 ± 250	7395 ± 258		31. I 715	8425 ± 275	8678 ± 283
7. GX 2243	7260 ± 320	7478 ± 330		32. GX 2809	8435 ± 500	8688 ± 515
8. P 1108	7287 ± 87	7506 ± 90		33. GX 2230	8480 ± 350	8734 ± 361
9. SI-2177	7360 ± 100	7581 ± 103				
10. GX 2246	7395 ± 160	7617 ± 165			*Hiatus (ash II)*	
11. SI-2180	7600 ± 100	7828 ± 103		34. SI-2178	9055 ± 95	9327 ± 98
12. P 1107	7657 ± 95	7887 ± 98		35. GX 2244	9805 ± 480	10099 ± 494
13. W 1180	7660 ± 300	7890 ± 309		Summary (Specimens 1 to 33)		
14. P 1102	7701 ± 93	7932 ± 96		Range	6992–8480	7202–8734
15. P 1837	7793 ± 116	8027 ± 119		Actual span	1488	1532
16. I 1046	7796 ± 230	8030 ± 237		Mean	7785	8019
17. GX 2234	7870 ± 260	8106 ± 268		S.D.	460.5	474.3
18. SI-2181	7885 ± 335	8122 ± 345		S.E.	80.5	82.6
19. SI-2175	7920 ± 100	8158 ± 103		Statistical		
20. P 1105	7932 ± 497	8170 ± 512		Range*	6864–8706	7070–8968
21. GX 2229	8055 ± 160	8297 ± 165		Statistical		
22. GX 2238	8060 ± 240	8302 ± 247		Span	1842	1898

* ± 2 S.D.
Source: Based on 33 specimens from between ashes II and III and two specimens directly on the ash II interface and below. The first specimen, GX 2232, is included to indicate the size of the ash III hiatus. Letter prefixes to specimen numbers denote the laboratory where the analysis was performed. Abbreviations: S.D., standard deviation of the mean; S.E., standard error of the mean.

terial culture underwent greater change than any other place in North America or Siberia, encompassing a change from unifacial tools to bifacial tools, and they demonstrate continuity of Aleut occupation through 9000 years on the shores of Nikolski Bay.

The analytical steps were developed over the years and all the evidence together forms a meaningful and fascinating picture of human history. All stages and phases of manufacture are represented here (Fig. 19). The maker began with a cobblestone or a lump of obsidian. This is the core, or nucleus (a). He struck some flakes with a hammerstone from the top to prepare a striking platform (b), and then he proceeded to strike blades from the sides of the core. After the removal of the outer surface of the original core, or cortex (c), the successive courses of blades (also termed *lamelles*) became prismatic in cross section (d). These prismatic blades were then used as scrapers and knives. They had very sharp edges, and some were retouched with flaking on one or both margins, but only on one surface. They are therefore called unifacial. As the striking platform became battered, it was "rejuvenated" by the removal of flakes [(e) and Fig. 20], and the core became shorter as well as smaller in circumference (f).

A few of the blades are pointed, some naturally and some by means of retouching on two margins of one surface (Fig. 21). There is only a hint of a shoulder or a stem that might have been used for hafting in a harpoon or arrow or as a graver on a few of the pointed specimens.

Another especially interesting tool is the Anangula burin. Sometimes whole blades were used, but more often a large blade was notched, then snapped into two or three segments. A transverse blow was then struck across the end to leave an inside edge that could be used, we assume, for softening skins (Fig. 22). Two

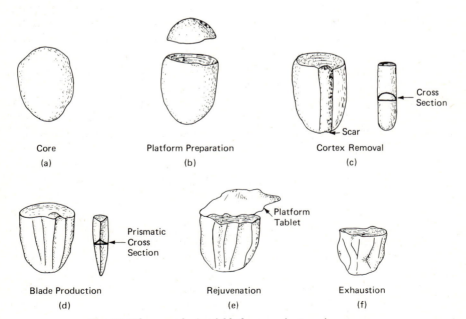

Fig. 19. Phase analysis of blade manufacture from cores.

Fig. 20. A core (5 cm. across) excavated in 1963 at the old Anangula site by A. P. McCartney, M. Yoshizaki, R. K. Nelson, and W. S. Laughlin. Tablet flakes, struck off the platform to rejuvenate its striking surface, have been reassembled. They show the way in which this core was reduced in size as prismatic blades were struck off and the striking platform was successively rejuvenated.

major kinds are angle burins and transverse burins. Both kinds were probably hafted in wood or bone handles. Some are made with a right-hand blow, if the smooth surface is held toward the maker, and some are made with a left-hand blow (Fig. 23).

The large number of stone artifacts is amazing. They mark this as the largest site in northern America or Siberia. The minimum measurements of the site are 100 meters by 250 meters. An average of 115 tools and flakes (excluding flake clusters) is found in each square meter. Therefore, no less than 2,875,000 stone artifacts are deposited here. About one-third of the Blade Site has been washed out into the Bering Sea.

The strata in which the tools are found is usually between 20 and 30 centimeters in thickness. The bone, ivory, and wood artifacts have long since decomposed in this acidulous soil and the formerly deep village deposits have been compressed to a small thickness of their original depth. Fifteen hundred years in the Chaluka midden or in the Anangula village midden consists of debris two to four meters in depth, depending on the durability of its composition.

Since this tail is a narrow finger-like projection, there were probably only 50 to 60 people living at this place at any one time, and, of course, it was only one village in a larger chain of villages. As a hunting station, it commanded both Nikolski Bay and the Bering Sea, and sampled all the resources of the area except for salmon, which were easily available in two streams across the bay. Fortunately,

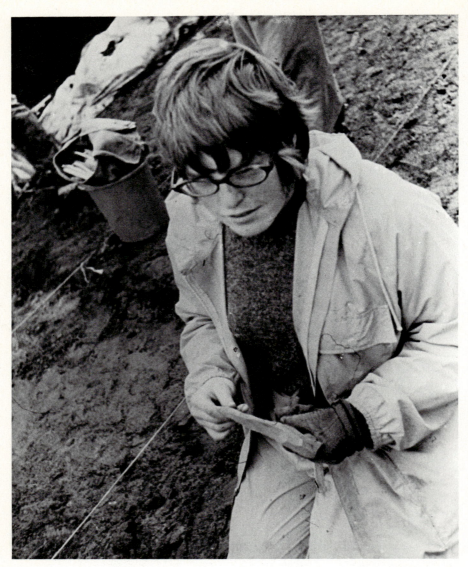

Fig. 21. Anangula, 1970. A large (18 cm.) prismatic blade just excavated by Sara B. Laughlin in the Anangula Blade Site (8700–7200 years ago). These blades are unifacial, with flake scars and retouching on only one surface.

the abundant obsidian tools prove that they maintained contact with the source of that excellent flaking material at Chagak on the northwest coast of Umnak Island.

The large number of radiocarbon specimens hints at the numbers of firehearths, but we have been unable to define the margins of houses and cannot estimate them. Three large houses could have accommodated all the villagers at any one time. The compaction of this village under the weight of ash and soil over the millennia has flattened 1500 years of village activities into one blanket of tools less than a third of a meter in thickness. The third dimension has been reduced by weight and time, but the horizontal relations have been undisturbed. Clusters of tools, cores, hammerstones, blades, and other products remain where they were left.

Melting glaciers caused sea levels to rise. Between about 10,000 years and 5000 years ago, the sea was rising rapidly enough that a man could see the difference in his lifetime. The low-lying tail of Anangula was subjected to more frequent drenching, especially in winter storm surges, and the people were forced to move to higher ground. They moved uphill to the village site. The sequence of natural events formed a Jacob's ladder, leading from lower to higher and earlier to later. The rungs of this "ladder" are the marine terrace (originally cut underwater and then raised), the volcanic ash layers, the unifacial tools in the lower site, the bifacial tools in the upper site, and the radiocarbon dates. Thus elevation, tool types, and radiocarbon dates establish the long history of the Aleuts in this bay. The tools by themselves tell only a part of the story.

After the people moved uphill, the Blade Site was preserved from further wave destruction of the rising sea by tectonic uplift that raised the island about 10 to 12 meters and exposed the marine terrace. However, at 18 meters above the sea the site was still not high enough for year-round occupation (see Fig. 24).

Volcanic eruptions are common in the Aleutian Islands and the ashes they emit provide time markers over large areas. Therefore, they provide a sound method for calibrating different archeological sites. From 1962–1963 a geologist, R. F. Black, appreciated the utility of volcanic ash layers and assigned numbers to four

Fig. 22. Three basic stone tools of the old Anangula Blade Site: a large unifacial prismatic blade, a double-ended burin made on a segment of a blade, and a core from which blades were struck.

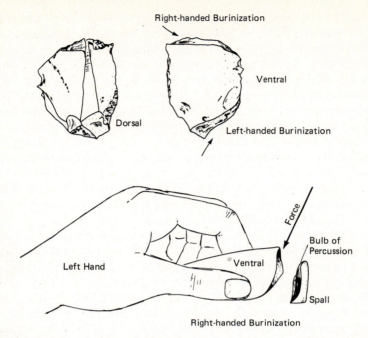

Fig. 23. Anangula Blade Site, 1972. A double burin: left- and right-handed buriniza-tion on one blade.

especially prominent layers. He also identified a more minor but nicely marked "key" ash (Fig. 25). Black's excellent identifications linked different sites together and the ashes are now well dated from the firehearth specimens in the archeological sites. The village mound of Chaluka, seven kilometers across Nikolski Bay, is effectively laminated with ash IV, and is underlain by ashes III, II, and I.

The Aleuts were familiar with volcanic eruptions. One of their stories concerns the owner or master of Okmok Crater on the north end of Umnak Island, and the master of Makushin Volcano on the neighboring island of Unalaska. They fought with each other for a long period of time, but the master of Okmok lost the contest when he blew out his top in a large eruption that left a great crater, or caldera. This great eruption is possibly one that deposited ash IV some 3000 years ago.

These eruptions may have caused the Aleut villages close by to move farther away, but if Okmok is the offending volcano, it probably had little effect on the Aleuts or on the lemmings who were 96 kilometers away. The supply of obsidian from Chagak on the slopes of Okmok appears to have continued uniformly in the villages of Nikolski Bay.

ANANGULA VILLAGE: TRANSITION CULTURE

The excavations of the Anangula Blade Site culminated in 1974 with the joint researches of a U.S.–U.S.S.R. field party (Fig. 26). Academician A. P. Okladnikov, discoverer of the Neanderthal child of Teshik Tash, with over 40 years of experience in all parts of Siberia and in Mongolia as well, excavated with me at the Blade Site (Fig. 27). Soviet scientists were well aware of the significance of Anangula, its stone tools and their relationship to Siberia, and its position at the end of the Bering Land Bridge. They knew where the first Americans came from and they wanted to know where they went. We knew where they had gone and wanted to know more about where they came from. These excavations were productive in stone tools, radiocarbon dates, tool distribution, stratigraphy, and other contextual data necessary for interpretation.

We now knew that the earliest Aleuts took up residence on the tail of Anangula when the sea level was much lower and that they began with a large cultural inventory. They had seal oil lamps, carved stone dishes, grinding stones and pallets for grinding red ochre pigments, line weights for fish lines, lava abraders for smoothing the wood shafts of harpoons, arrows, boat members and other things of wood and bone, unifacial obsidian scrapers for scraping sea mammal and bird skins in addition to the burin, blade, and core industry. These same traits are also found in the later Aleut culture of Chaluka, the old village mound across the Bay at Nikolski within eyesight. The persistence of these traits over a period of 8700 years indicated a genuine continuity of culture on this Bay. However, the period between 7000 and 4000 years ago was not actually filled in with artifacts and dates. The missing link in this chain of prehistory was discovered, unexpectedly, exactly where it belonged.

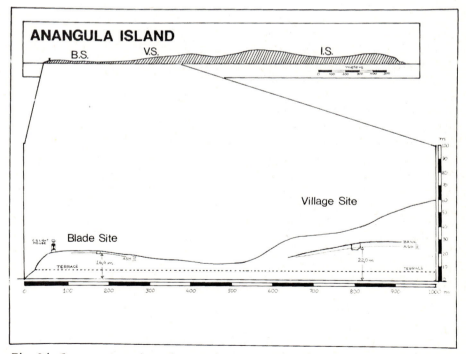

Fig. 24. Cross-section of southern end of Anangula Island, showing elevations of the Blade Site and the Village Site.

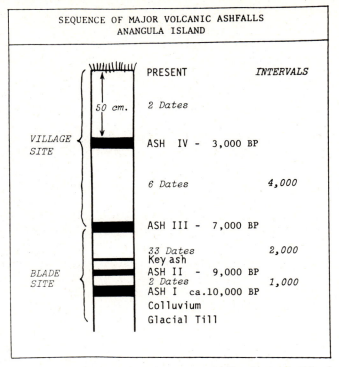

Fig. 25. Sequence of major volcanic ashfalls, Anangula Island.

The Village Site, which is higher on the side of Anangula facing Nikolski, is only half a kilometer from the Blade Site. Okladnikov and I decided to examine it in the few remaining days. Four of us (Okladnikov, Rusland Vasilievsky, Sasha Konopatskij, and I) removed the hummocks of green grass from an area on the brow of the old village, rolling them down on to the terrace below, and proceeded to shovel and trowel into the mound. We found bones of seals, sea lions, cormorants, and albatross and tools of the later Aleut culture of the last 3000 years. Suddenly Okladnikov shouted, "Plastina," and held up a prismatic blade (Fig. 28). It was a tool typical of the Blade Site in the lower levels of the Village Site. Fifteen minutes later, he stupefied us with another stone tool held up high, and the words, "Ushki chereskowi" (Fig. 28). He had found a bifacially-flaked point, similar in some respects to those found at Lake Ushki on the Kamchatka Peninsula. A few more days of rain and digging produced burins, cores, blades, long bifacial points with short stems, and short bifacial points with long stems all down in the lower levels between 7000 and 4000 years ago (Fig. 29). The two vital missing links had been found by Okladnikov, a prismatic blade from the older industry and a bifacial blade from the newer industry. These two technologies overlapped and integrated with each other for a long period of transition in which the older industry declined and the newer technology became dominant.

Fortunately, bone tools began to appear in the last 6000 years, and with them the

Fig. 26. Anangula, 1974. The joint Soviet–United States party excavating the old unifacial blade, burin, and core site on Anangula. Several layers of volcanic ash overlie the cultural horizon. Some 9000 artifacts came from the exposure seen here.

bones of the birds, fish, and sea mammals interbedded with sea urchin remains. This village continued in active use into the nineteenth century, and later was used for summer camp. The halibut fishing beds on the shallow bay side and in Seaweed Pass between Anangula and Umnak are a favorite fishing place for Aleuts who regularly land many halibut on handlines. One old lady told of many summers spent here with a family who caught and dried halibut and then returned to Nikolski in the fall when the village was red with drying salmon. An informative discovery was a nicely fashioned harpoon head found by Sara Laughlin underneath a rock in the cove at Anangula. It precisely matches a harpoon head found in the upper levels of the village excavations. This is one of the styles, made of the jawbone of a whale, that was in use when the first Russians arrived in the eighteenth century.

The surface of the Village Site is indented with 24 house pits arranged in three irregular rows along 125 meters of the crest of the bluff. A dense cover of monks-hood or aconite (*Aconitum maximum*) and ryegrass (*Elymus mollis*) blankets the entire village. Directly behind the village, there are several mounds enclosed in V-shaped trenches. In each case, the apex of the V is uphill and was intended to drain water away from the protected mound. These mounds, called *umqan*, were used for burials (Fig. 30).

Fig. 27. Anangula, 1974. Soviet academician A. P. Okladnikov holds a transverse burin; Mrs. W. S. Laughlin records it in the log book. Such burins are a common feature of the Anangula blade culture and are similar to those in Japan and Siberia.

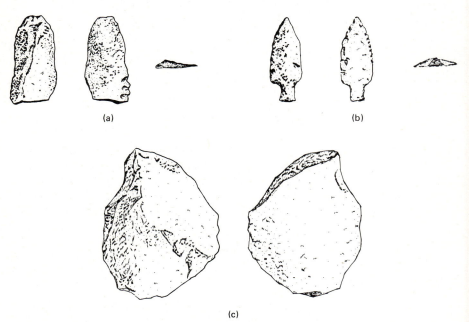

(a)   (b)

(c)

Fig. 28. Stone tools from the transition culture of Anangula Village (natural size). (a) Prismatic blade with some retouching on dorsal surface. (b) Bifacial, stemmed point. Though genuinely bifacial, the point appears to have been made on a prismatic blade. The stem remains triangular in cross-section and one surface of the point is flat with retouching confined to the margins. (c) Angle burin made on a broad lamellar flake.

Fig. 29. Bifacially flaked projectile points of the Transition Culture, Anangula Village Site. The smaller point has a long shank or stem; the larger point has a relatively short stem. Prior to this time (6000 or more years ago), all the stone tools were unifacial.

ALEUT ORIGINS ON THE BERING LAND BRIDGE

The Bering Land Bridge formerly connected Siberia to Alaska. It was a broad, low, treeless tundra or steppe, and was very cold and dry. The north side of the Bridge, fronting on the Arctic Ocean, was permanently frozen the year round and no hunting was possible. The middle of the Land Bridge was suitable although difficult for hunting land animals, such as caribou, mammoth, antelope, and musk ox. The ancestors of the American Indians probably moved through the interior, following the migratory animals. However, the ancestors of the Aleuts and Eskimos more likely moved along the southern coastline, developing the knowledge necessary to exploit the richer and more stable marine environment and maintaining permanent villages (Figs. 31 and 32).

Eventually, the great continental ice sheets began to melt and return their waters to the oceans. With this melting, the world's sea levels rose. The Bering Land Bridge, or Beringia as it is sometimes called, was submerged. By 13,000 years ago at least one channel was exposed between the Chukchi Peninsula of Siberia and St. Lawrence Island, and 1–2000 years later another channel was exposed between St. Lawrence and the Seward Peninsula of Alaska. Those people living in the interior of Beringia were forced to move. In contrast, the people living on the southern coast of the Land Bridge and at the mouths of the great rivers that emptied

Fig. 30. Leslie Laughlin and Bruno Frøhlich excavating umqan *burial of Village Site, Anangula. Excavation of earlier unifacial blade and core site is seen at lower elevation about .5 km. south in the background.*

into it—the Yukon and the Kuskokwim—remained on the coast and enjoyed the increase in coastline.

There is an Asiatic template in the Aleutians that persists through time. It could only have come off the Land Bridge from sites now submerged. Those sites found at the present base of the Alaska Peninsula and Kodiak Island are quite different in their beginning technological phases. They also lack lamps, stone dishes, and other traits that are continuous in Aleutian prehistory. They probably represent the earliest Eskimo culture.

All the first Americans were skilled hunters when they entered the New World.

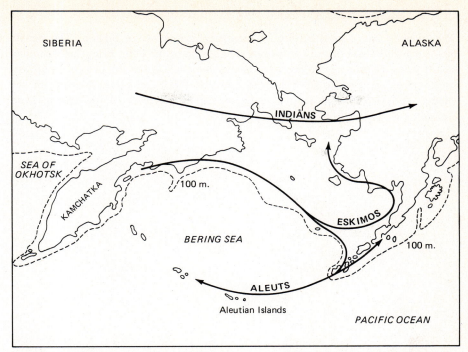

Fig. 31. *Ancestors of the American Indians migrated through the interior of the Bering Land Bridge. Ancestors of the Aleuts and Eskimos followed the southern coast and diverged from each other in southwestern Alaska.*

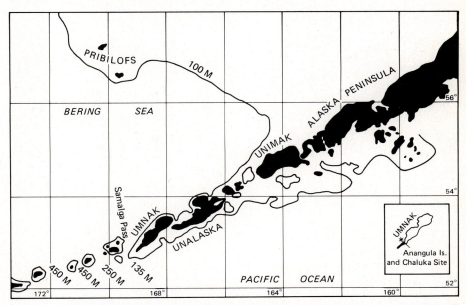

Fig. 32. *Earlier coastline of the Bering Land Bridge 11–12,000 years ago. Umnak Island was then the terminus of the Alaska Peninsula. Samalga Pass, between Kagamil and Umnak Islands, was then the easternmost pass channeling whales, fur seals, and fish from the Pacific Ocean into the Bering Sea (courtesy of R. F. Black).*

They already had a long history of successful adaptation in Siberia. The people who reached the end of the southwestern extension of the Land Bridge at Anangula clearly had a diverse culture and were able to remain there to the present by adjusting their village sites to the changing coastline. The distinctive character of the Aleuts stems from their distinctive beginning as survivors of the Bering Land Bridge.

7 / Chaluka: the last 4000 years of Aleut history

A large, oval green mound rises gently from the low-lying land between Umnak Lake and Nikolski Bay (Fig. 33). This is the ancient village of Chaluka; it chronicles the last 4000 years of Aleut history from the early sea-mammal hunters who lived in stone-based houses in the lower levels to their modern descendants, who live above ground and who still fish in the same waters, but who now keep as watchful an eye on Washington, D.C., as they do on Nikolski Bay. Chaluka is the southern portion of Nikolski and the name is used for the local village corporation.

This mound, or midden, is some 215 meters long, 61 meters wide, and 8 meters in its deepest parts. It is composed of occupational debris that includes much shell from sea urchins, mussels, limpets, whelks, and chitons; volcanic ash, earth, stones, and charcoal; fish, bird, and sea-mammal bones; house floors and walls; tools of stone, bone, and ivory; and burials—in short, of everything the Aleuts left behind, including themselves. The skin and basketry materials, the sinew bindings and intestine pouches, birdskin parkas, wood dishes, and ladles have all disappeared except for rare cases where peat or fine clay has sealed out the air and preserved the wood. The chemical richness of this mound, especially in nitrogen, encourages a diverse group of plants. Hundreds of such village mounds in the Aleutians can be detected by their greener and denser vegetation. Aleut men formerly raised potatoes and onions in little garden plots on village sites. Aleut women use soil from Chaluka for their house plants.

Perhaps the first European to see this old village was Glotov, who is credited with discovering Umnak Island in 1759. Later, in July of 1764 A.D., Korovin buried the bodies of the Medvedev party in the western end of Chaluka facing the inner bay. They had been massacred earlier that year by a federation of Aleuts at Chaluka. These burials establish a valuable time marker as well as a commentary on the nature of the relations between Aleuts and Cossacks (see Chapter 10). A chapel was established on the eastern end of Chaluka in 1795 or 1799, a sod-covered *barabara*. It was later rebuilt as a frame building and moved across to the north side of Umnak Creek, where it was enlarged and stands today. Waldemar Jochelson spent several months here in 1909, excavating in other village sites and studying the customs, history, and language. His wife took anthropological measurements. It is significant that Jochelson did not excavate in Chaluka, and, therefore, missed a great deal of early Paleo-Aleut history. The reason is that most of the Aleuts were still living on top of Chaluka.

Chaluka was one of 22 villages on Umnak Island proper. Nikolski is now the

Fig. 33. Nikolski, Umnak Island. The old village midden of Chaluka spans 4000 years. Umnak Lake lies immediately behind it; Mueller Cove of Nikolski Bay lies in front.

sole remaining village. Within the past 125 years only two of these original 22 villages have been inhabited. Nikolski, the first, was earlier named Rechesnoi on Russian charts. The second remaining village, Tulik Village on the northeast end of the island near the offshore Ship Rock Island, is where some of its inhabitants were mummified and interred. In addition to the 22 villages on Umnak Island, there were three on Samalga Island, at the far south end of Umnak, one on Anangula Island, and a permanent summer residence on Vsevidof Island, which lies off the southeast coast of Umnak opposite the old village of Uyu, whose inhabitants utilized this island. In modern Aleut tradition, Chaluka was a large village before the coming of the whites, containing a population of 200 or maybe 300. It was one of the five largest Umnak villages. The other four were Tulik Village on Otter Point, Adhush on the northern end of the island near the mouth of Crater Creek, Qumningan on the south shore of Inanudak Bay, and Aglaga on the southwest tip of Umnak. The total population of Umnak is estimated at 2000 to 2500 Aleuts.

TOOLS FOR MAKING A LIVING

Among the tools for making a living were those associated with hunting, fishing, fowling, and root digging. The fishing implements consisted of grooved stones used as line weights or sinkers. Larger stones of 4 kilograms or more were probably used as weights for netting fish and sea mammals. Fishhooks were compound—that is, they were made of two parts, a shank and a barb, the barb, in turn, having smaller barbs on it. Early-style shanks were shaped like an elbow and carved from whale-bone. Later styles were simply fashioned from ribs. The barbs were beautifully made, in some cases of ivory rather than bone. Long lines, as much as 60 fathoms, were made from kelp. Dr. R. Lyapunova and I took a rough measurement of one in the Leningrad collections. It had 103 loops, each 70 centimeters in length, for a total line length of 72 meters. Eleven pieces had been tied together to make this fish line. The stone sinker was secured on a separate line and attached to the main line so that the sinker rested on the floor of the ocean with the hook floating above the sinker. Compound fishhooks ranged in size from large ones used for halibut to small ones used in shallowed waters for sculpin and cod.

Fish spears ordinarily had slender or pointed bases and were themselves more slender overall than those for sea mammals. The leister was an interesting kind of fishing spear which had two side prongs that slipped over the sides of a fish, while the pointed central spear point impaled the fish. These were used especially along the banks of streams and lakes for trout and salmon, and on the reef for catching kelp fish such as greenling, though a net on a pole might be used in preference. The two side prongs were made of springy wood and carried the bone "catch." These were not found in the early levels. Simple slivers of bone, "gorges," were also attached to a line and used for catching small fish, often by small boys.

Sea-mammal hunting was responsible for a fascinating array of harpoon heads with much decoration. A basic form of a large harpoon head was fluted, or chan-neled on its sides, with small barbs, and a large end slot to receive a chipped stone point [see H-3 in Fig. 34 and (a) in Fig. 35]. The blunt base is smaller than the barrel of the head, flat, and may have been inserted directly into a wood shaft without benefit of a bone socket-piece. This kind or class of harpoon head was used for large sea mammals such as the sea lion. One rare example of the chipped stone end point, embedded in the humerus (upper arm bone) of a sea lion shows the force with which these harpoons were cast. Small whales, yearlings and calves, were probably hunted with these harpoon heads. A second basic form was broad with two barbs, one larger than the other, and had a line hole in the base [see H-4 in Fig. 34 and (b) in Fig. 35]. This line hole provided the point of attachment for a braided sinew line that went either to the wood shaft or to a float. This type also used an inset stone end point. A few toggle harpoon heads were found at all levels. These had a slot for a stone point and a line hole. After penetrating the animal, the head responded to the line tension by turning at right angles to the line, and an attached foreshaft dropped out of the socket piece to give it additional freedom. Northern Eskimo cultures used many more toggle-head harpoons than the simple, detachable styles favored in the Aleutians.

The form of these harpoon heads in themselves constituted art styles. As a tendency, early harpoon heads more often were asymmetrical than later heads. The barbs were frequently larger on one side than the other, and commonly, the smaller barbs were thinner and more sharply delineated. A common incised decoration for harpoon heads was a circle and a dot, often with a line running through it. One charming Mongoloid face was carved on the base of a harpoon head, employ-ing the line hole as its mouth. In late styles, the sides of harpoon heads were some-times decorated with faces.

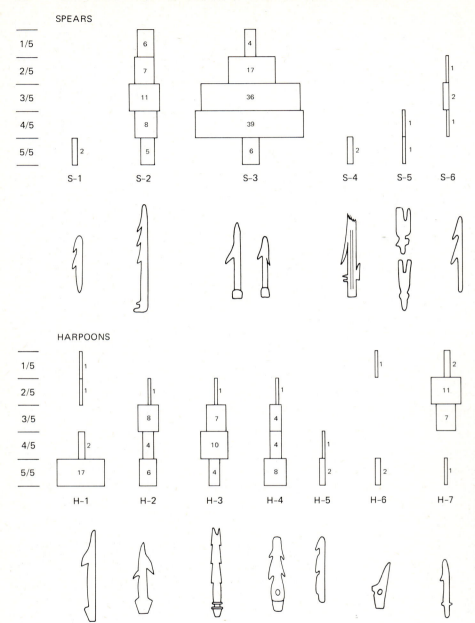

Fig. 34. Depth distribution chart of the classes of spearheads and harpoon heads from the Chaluka site, Umnak Island.

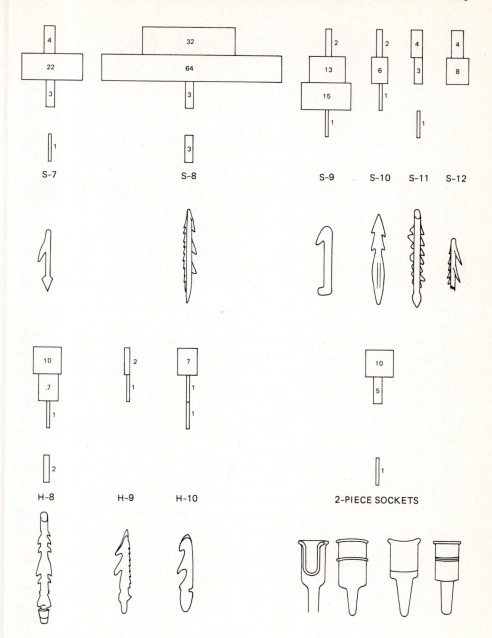

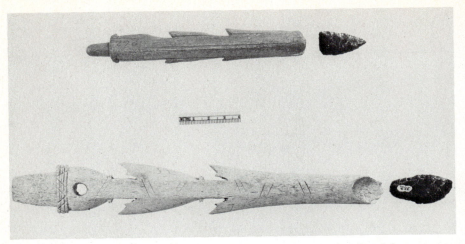

Fig. 35. Early and late harpoon styles. (a) The early style is fluted and has a square based slot for insertion of a square based endpoint. (b) The later style (in use when the Russians arrived) has a rounded basin for insertion of a round-based endpoint.

Fowling was represented by three-pronged spears that were secured to a wood shaft when in use. In ethnographic specimens (collected from Aleuts who actually used them), two kinds were found—those with barbs pointed inward and those with barbs directed outward. Whether they were used for different kinds of birds or simply by different persons who preferred one kind over the other is not recorded. Both kinds are known archeologically, and the earliest (see S-2 in Fig. 34) were usually made of ivory with the barbs turned outward. This type of spearhead has been in continuous use for 4000 years. The later style has the larger barbs on the inside facing the central spearhead point.

Sets of eight girdled stones suggested the use of the bolas for catching birds. The bolas was ordinarily made with several uniform weights of ivory, stone, or bone, each on a sinew line of roughly 40 centimeters in length. Thrown into a flight of birds, it would entangle one or more and was especially useful for ducks and geese where the ducks are landing or taking off and, therefore, are still close to land.

An interesting change, one of many which had no apparent relation to the efficacy of hunting, was the change both in spears and harpoons in the method of inserting the end point. End points in the earlier harpoon heads were usually inserted into a slot, whereas end points of later harpoon heads were more often inserted into a basin on the side of the harpoon head. This changeover took place at the same time that two-piece sockets made their definitive appearance. Whereas most socket pieces were made of a single piece of fine-grained bone or ivory, these were made of two pieces, bilaterally symmetrical but separate longitudinally. The most exotic example [see H-8 in Fig. 34 and (a) and (b) in Fig. 36] was a late style (no more than 1000 years ago), that was still known to the Aleuts at contact. The head was inserted in a two-piece socket and lashed to the wood shaft so that it was not detachable. Technically, it was a lance head when mounted in this way.

It was suitable for both whales and humans, since it was long enough to reach from the chest to the spine of a man.

Plant foods were a small but important part of the Aleut diet. Unfortunately, plants leave no skeletons. Fortunately, the root digger, a curved shaft of whalebone, that was sometimes decorated, continued in use and the archeological specimens were easily identified. The use of invertebrates—sea urchins, limpets, whelks, clams, mussels, and chitons—is established by the presence of invertebrate shells in village debris. Some of the bird bone awls—those with broad ends—were used for prying meat from the shell. Such tools are not necessary, however, since one limpet shell can be used to disinter the occupant of another.

TOOLS FOR MAKING TOOLS

Among the tools for making tools, the most important were often the least interesting. The hammerstone initiated the entire process of detaching flakes from cores, either lamellar or random according to period and preference. The hammer-

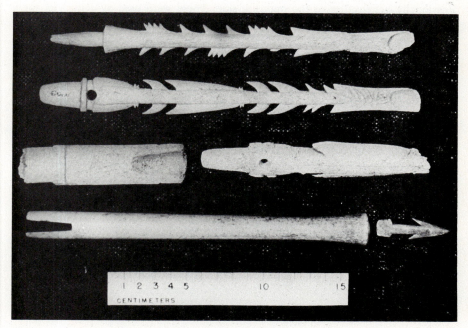

Fig. 36. Late-style harpoon heads. (a) This specimen has a round basin for a chipped stone endpoint. (b) Another style with a round basin for a chipped stone endpoint. This whalebone head was used in fighting and was then secured to the shaft, converting it technically to a lance or spear. (c) One half of a two-piece socket illustrates the method of seating this harpoon head. (d) The small detachable point is designed for sea otter hunting. The whalebone socket piece has a slot for the insertion of the tongue of the wood shaft. This style was most common after Russian contact.

stone of quartzite or other hard rock also served for pecking the basin in seal oil lamps and pecking girdles in sinkers and weights for bolas. After the basin of a lamp was pecked out, the final stages of polishing were accomplished with sand, and even the siliceous horsetail rush (*Equisetum*) was used.

After a flake (spall) was detached and perhaps roughly shaped by the hammerstone, it was then pressure-flaked with a narrow, pointed piece of bone. The two most common forms were simply pointed ends of ribs, frequently sea otter ribs. The earlier style was more blunt than the later one. Another kind of flaker was cut from whalebone, some 15 centimeters in length and rectangular in cross section. This was lashed to a wood or bone handle. A projectile point was chipped while it was held in the palm of the hand, first the tip and then the base. Incomplete specimens show that this method was used from the earliest times to the present for bifacial points. The stem of the Aleut word for "chipping," "flaking," or "retouching" is also the stem of the word for "hand." As with many techniques of manufacture, the technique could have been inferred from the Aleut word.

The most common wood-working tool was the simple whalebone wedge. Hundreds of these attest to the importance of splitting wood throughout the Aleutians, as well as at Chaluka, and for all periods. Many of them had polished circular pits, occasionally penetrating to the opposite side. These were used as drill rests for a drill operated with a bow to start fires and to drill holes. After the Russians arrived, a flywheel was added to the shaft that carried the stone drill point, and metal points replaced chipped stone points. The simple bow and string were replaced with the newly introduced yoke, with strings going to the top of the shaft. These were used well into this century.

Adze blades and the whalebone adzeheads into which they were fitted were found in the Chaluka village debris. The adze bits varied in size from small and narrow, like chisels, to large and broad. This was the basic wood-shaping and -carving tool for masks, boat members, house timbers, dishes, hats, and cradle frames. Scrapers, knives, and drills completed the list of those wood-working tools with cutting edges. Mauls were essential to the use of wedges.

Abraders made of scoriaceous lava or of pumice were used for shaping and polishing the shafts of harpoons, harpoon head sheaths, arrows, handles, and many other objects made of wood. Many of the same abraders and polishing stones were also used for working bone and ivory. Most of the ivory came from the sperm whale tooth, some from other toothed whales. Occasionally walrus ivory was traded out into the Aleutian chain. Stone saws and heavy knives with chipped and serrated teeth were used for cutting bone and some soft stone.

SKIN WORKING

Skin-dressing tools prominently included chipped stone semilunar blades and many chipped stone blades that were simply a point made by chipping two edges of a piece of basalt without continuing on around to form a chipped back or handle area. The semilunar forms were often called *ulus* in the Eskimo tradition. These tools were used by women who did the skin working, but women also used such knives for cleaning fish and skinning the sea mammals brought in by Aleut men. Other important tissues used for clothing were the intestines, the skin of the whale tongue, the pericardium, and the throat (esophagus). Needles, awls (some made from sea otter leg bones but usually of bird bone), scrapers, and semilunar knives (for which the Aleut use the same stem word as for "the place for making stone-blades," *igan*) were the essential tools for working skins into clothes and boat covers. Pumice abraders were used for smoothing and thinning the hides after the fat had been removed.

Aside from the skin-dressing tools and the root diggers, there is little evidence of women's activities except for the substantial beds of shells. However, the mummy caves at Kagamil were filled with numerous examples of the women's fine ability in weaving and basketry. Since men were concerned with hunting, boating, and the manufacture of tools—all of which required extensive equipment and some of which was of relatively imperishable materials—it becomes obvious that the importance of women's activities cannot be measured by the number of artifacts they left behind. In this respect, at least, the Aleut world was a man's world. The sexual division of labor and of proceeds was both ancient and ubiquitous.

The most common chipped stone knife had a tang that was inserted into a handle. This was the man's knife. It is possible that an antecedent form occurred in the Anangula core and blade culture, although the shoulder of the tang was only lightly developed. These knives were carried by men, sometimes inside the sleeve as was done during the attack on the Medvedev Russians (see Chapter 10). It was the basic tool for skinning animals, for carving, and for a variety of tasks.

DIVERSE OBJECTS

Lamps and pots were found throughout Chaluka. The early stone lamps had thick bottoms and walls, and the oil basin was flush at one end. The later styles were thin-bottomed with a low rim that encircled the perimeter equally on all sides. They were often made of soapstone and were usually shallow. This style was also found in the mummy caves. Ordinary boulders with a natural depression were also identified as lamps by the carbon deposits in their basins. Pots or carved stone dishes—not to be confused with pottery which did not occur—were deeper than lamps. The walls and bottoms of the pots were of uniform thickness. The carbon deposit was on the ouside. Household lamps were tended by women and, since they did most of the cooking, these objects provided evidence of women's functions.

Images of the deity were found in Chaluka and as a direct consequence, our knowledge of old Aleut religious beliefs has been enriched. They were little figures of human shape made of ivory, bone, or stone. A groove around the head and over the middle provided a girdle for suspension from the ceiling beam of a house. They were used into the nineteenth century. The hunter would speak to this personification of the deity before undertaking sea voyages, and would, in turn, be spoken to by the deity. The Aleut name *kaadagaadagh* is derived from the stem for a deity with the addition of a diminutive ending. It clearly indicates that this is a small image of the larger deity. A related figure, in sitting position, was seen on some wood hunting hats in ethnographic collections. The archeological discovery of the first image of the deity in 1948 elicited linguistic and cultural information that would otherwise have gone unstudied. Inhibitions on discussions of such topics in the time of Veniaminov and later periods had virtually concealed this important area. A native Aleut, Mr. A. K. Ermeloff, identified the image of the deity as well as many other artifacts.

HOUSES

The earliest people at Chaluka made houses in a style quite different from the later *barabaras*. They were constructed with walls of large stones or boulders set on edge, and by walls of stone laid flat upon each other (Fig. 37). There has not been enough excavation to describe entrances and roofing in any detail. The presence of a large whale mandible over one of these houses suggests that they had been raftered with bone as well as with driftwood timbers. The large stones set on end or on edge in a circular or oval outline occurred on the bottom soil and could have been used for tents, possibly double-walled tents. The more massive

Fig. 37. East end of Chaluka, 1971. A 4000-year-old stone-based house.

coursed walls, on the other hand, could represent more durable houses. The later *barabaras* (a Siberian term introduced by the Russians) were dug into the ground and used much planking in the walls as well as wood rafters with some whalebone. They did not use stone walls or stone-based walls. The roof was covered with matting and then with sod. Houses of the last several hundred years were large, rectangular, with a roof entry way, and infrequently had open-fire hearths. Lamps were used for light, heat, and cooking.

BURIALS

All the inhabitants of Chaluka, as well as of the entire Aleut area, were buried in a flexed position and lying on one side until the establishment of Russian Orthodox cemeteries. Red ochre stained the heads of many Paleo-Aleuts and raw chunks of ochre were occasionally included with the grave goods. All sexes and ages were found in burials (Fig. 38). Young children sometimes had beads buried with them, as indicated by a child's grave that included small amber beads. Amber occurs on Umnak Island and was systematically mined during the Russian period by shoveling the amber-bearing earth down onto skins spread out from the large, open *baidars*.

The diversity in grave furnishing was ingenious. Burials have been found on top of a large whale scapula (shoulder blade), inside a box made of flat stones, with chunks of whalebone lying over the skeleton, and sometimes including harpoon heads, labrets, and a lamp, but more often containing nothing. Facets on the lower teeth show which persons wore labrets. A utilization of whale bone was clearly indicated and we inferred that whales had always been hunted, although a whale that had died of natural causes and drifted ashore could not be distinguished from one that had been lanced and towed ashore.

The skeletons themselves yielded three basic and indispensable categories of information. They demonstrated the genetic continuity with living Aleuts, most readily apparent in the dentition, and therefore, proved that Aleuts have been the exclusive occupants and owners of the area. They provided the basic demographic information on age at death and therefore of life expectancy. It is important to appreciate that the Aleuts had achieved a high life expectancy before European intrusion and acculturation. The skeletons also reflected an internal change in the population, namely, the passage from the earlier, more narrow-headed form to the broad-headed form. At present, this change in vault form (primarily the brain case exclusive of the face and mandible) appears to represent an evolutionary change within the Aleut population system that is comparable to the same direction of change in all other parts of the world (see Chapter 2).

FAUNAL REMAINS

Chaluka, like other Aleutian village sites, is especially informative because the remains of the animals hunted and eaten by the people are well preserved. From

Fig. 38. Nikolski, 1961. Mr. Leon Ermeloff excavates the skeleton of an elderly lady in the Chaluka mound.

the historical and ethnographic accounts, it is clear that the sea lion was the most sought after sea mammal. This appears to be substantiated by the faunal remains. At Chaluka, the sea lion bones usually comprised 10 to 20 percent of sea mammal bones, closer to 10 percent when sea otters were included, and closer to 20 percent when only pinnipeds (sea lion, hair seal, and fur seal) were counted. Estimating the average sea lion at 454 kilograms and a seal or sea otter at 40–45 kilograms, the sea lion provided as much meat as all the other sea mammals together, excluding whales, porpoises, and dolphins.

Sea otter bones showed a substantial rise in the Russian period, a response to the increase in sea otter hunting. Sea otters apparently did not taste very good. According to one experienced Aleut, they tasted like mud. Their magnificent fur, however, was used for women's clothing. There was also an increase in fox bones, undoubtedly engendered by commercial trapping. A few dog bones also appeared during the Russian period and an occasional caribou bone that had been traded out from the eastern area, Unimak Island, the Alaska Peninsula, or one of the islands in the Shumagin group.

Birds have always been one of the mainstays of Aleut life. It is interesting that albatrosses are well represented in village debris, since they must usually be caught at sea. The bird bone inventory for Chaluka was especially interesting because most of the birds had to be caught elsewhere and brought there. In a sample of 3985 bird bones (each represented one bird) from both east and west Chaluka, 5 percent were albatross (*Diomedeidae*), 40 percent were shearwaters and fulmars (*Procellariidae*), 9 percent were cormorants (*Phalacrocoracidae*), 10 percent were ducks (*Anaiidae*), 32 percent were puffins and auklets (*Alcidae*), and the remaining 4 percent comprised different families. Puffins were extensively used for clothing as well as for food, whereas cormorants were used for clothing but not as much for food. Fewer cormorant skins were needed for a garment, however, and their 9 percent is roughly proportional by this interpretation to the 32 percent sample content of puffins and auklets.

The interpretation of the faunal remains is excellent for demonstrating what animals were present and for rough correspondences with the Aleut hunting methods and their implementation. Unfortunately, when even a large number of sea mammal or bird bones is divided by 4000 years and stratigraphic partitions are recognized, it is more difficult to follow trends over time and to distinguish common fluctuations from availability at a particular village. The implications of increasing population size and trade are also difficult to track over vast stretches of time. The ancient Aleuts used all available foods, traveled whatever distance was necessary, and employed ingenious methods to secure their prey.

When the invertebrates are added to the archeological food list, the diversity of food resources becomes apparent. It is critically important that the invertebrates could be easily collected by most people, although women, children, and aged persons harvested a great deal of these foods from the reefs at low tide. Sea urchins were best represented, followed variously by limpets, mussels, chitons, whelks, and clams. Unfortunately, neither the octopus remains nor the marine algae that were generously used can be identified. Of the fish, halibut and cod last much better in the village deposits than do salmon and other smaller fish.

TRENDS IN CHIPPED STONE ARTIFACTS

Aleut culture underwent major changes in the form of their artifacts and in the techniques used to manufacture them. This cultural transition first became apparent when the kinds of tools in the lower parts of Chaluka were compared with those in the uppermost levels. The tools made on blades, earlier termed lamellar tools, were more frequent in the lowest levels. A significant amount of change was registered in the last 4000 years. When articulated chronologically with the earlier changes that took place across the Bay, it forms a documented picture of slow but dramatic change. The Aleuts passed from 100 percent dependence upon unifacial tools to nearly 100 percent dependence upon bifacially chipped tools. If the ground stone blades and points of recent times (about 2–300 years ago at Chaluka, but earlier at sites to the east, such as Akun Island) are added, the transformation is even more dramatic. In quantified form, the change is measurable, although only approximate:

TABLE 7.1.   CHANGE FROM UNIFACIAL TO BIFACIAL ARTIFACTS
(Measured at Chaluka and Anangula)

Location and Time Depth	Sample Size	Percent Unifacial	Percent Bifacial
Recent Chaluka (ca. 600 years ago)	70	6	94
Lower Chaluka (ca. 4–3000 years ago)	88	31	69
Transition Culture, Levels 3 and 4, Anangula (ca. 7–5000 years ago)	65	57	43
Prismatic Blade Site, Anangula (ca. 8700–7000 years ago)	20,000+	100	0

A NEWER VIEW OF THE HISTORY OF THE ALEUTIANS

The unique intercontinental position of the Aleutian Islands, forming a chain between Asia and the New World, has resulted in much discussion on the origin and affinities of the Aleuts. A paucity of sound anthropological data, together with the tantalizing proximity of the Commander Islands and Kamchatka, permitted the suggestion that the Aleuts followed this direct route from Asia to the Aleutian Islands rather than along the southern coast of the Bering Land Bridge.

In 1948, we began the excavation of Chaluka where Hrdlička had dug in 1938, with the belief that the Aleuts could have been there longer than 2000 years. We also had grounds to believe that Aleut culture was much more sophisticated and complex than ordinarily believed at that time. We pursued archeological studies simultaneously with linguistic, ethnographic, and physical anthropological studies of the Aleuts themselves.

There is an interesting reciprocity between these diverse studies. Some information is complementary and belongs equally in different disciplines. The image of the deity, for example, would remain an interesting archeological item, a charming art form at best, if the Aleut name, its meaning, and its use had not been correctly attached to it. Without the burials and skeletons, the change in physical type would have gone unnoticed as well as the basic demographic data on length of life and pathologies. Without the studies of living Aleuts, their measurements, blood groups, medical and dental facts, the skeletal evidence could not be adequately interpreted. In fact, neither the Aleuts nor the researchers could have proved that they were the genetic descendants of the people responsible for the artifacts, burials, faunal remains, and houses in the occupation sites.

By 1951, we had a 3000-year date, determined by Dr. W. F. Libby of the Institute for Nuclear Studies, University of Chicago, for samples of burned wood taken from a hearth one meter above the natural floor of the site. We therefore reasoned that the lowest level must be several hundred years older. A date of about 4000 years was assumed. There are now 44 radiocarbon dates for the Chaluka midden. They are, of course, not evenly distributed. In order to date the volcanic ash IV, we submitted more specimens from above and below the sterile ash than for some other strata. A single date, such as the 3000-year date, was useful but it was not demonstrably sound until several more dates were available to verify it.

In the same way, the first dates from the Anangula Blade Site were extremely valuable, but the scientific verification of them could only follow on a larger number of dates. The 33 dates now available are sufficient to demonstrate that there is over 90 percent certainty that the span of occupation (1500 years) of the core-and-blade site is correct as well as its chronology. With only three dates, we could be only about 10 percent certain. The Transition Culture, with only six dates, needs more dates to fill out the picture and provide a specifiable degree of confidence. Context, of course, is critically important. The Transition Culture is locked in between its earlier core-and-blade ancestor on the one hand and its later descendant forms on the other.

Calibration is an invaluable aid to articulating the human occupation of different sites. This purpose is served in Nikolski Bay by three things: (1) the record of sea level that must necessarily be the same for both sides of the same bay; (2) five identifiable volcanic ashes, each from a separate eruption, and all found on both sides of the bay; and (3) the types of tools that change with time but which are the same for both sides of the bay at any one time. The actual dating of artifacts depended upon radiocarbon dating to establish the time in which short-term events occurred, the span of occupation of the sites, and the many protracted events—such as the intermittent change in harpoon styles or the shift from unifacial to bifacial technology. The Russian skeletons in Chaluka are too late to be dated by radiocarbon methods, but the written records establish the date of the massacre in the spring of 1764 (see Chapter 10).

Anangula Island was a peninsula of Umnak Island 8700 years ago and was the northern arm of Nikolski Bay. Seaweed Pass, still very shallow today, had not yet been filled with water. Anangula did not become an island until about 6–7000 years ago. Modern sea level was established about 4–5000 years ago. The Chaluka occupation began after the modern sea level was stabilized. Now we know that the inner bay (Mueller Cove) did not exist prior to about 4500 years ago. At that time, the bay became considerably larger and enriched. Sea mammals and fish could enter from the north as well as from the south, and the exposed reefs supported a more abundant and accessible supply of invertebrates and reef fish. The site of Chaluka then became an ideal site for the Aleuts who could take advantage, simultaneously, of the salmon stream, the lakes, the reefs, and the protected inner bay, and enjoy rapid access to the outer bay and the Bering Sea. The bottom of Chaluka was not the beginning of Aleut history; it marks the beginning of the Aleuts living at Chaluka. Perhaps at this time, or earlier, the Aleuts began their expansion to the east and to the west.

The long history of the Aleuts can now be assembled in its major features and the last 4000 years in considerable detail. The earliest people moved out to Nikolski Bay at the end of the southwestern extension of the Bering Land Bridge. They probably had to boat across narrow channels that began the partitioning of the old Peninsula into major island clusters, and possibly they had to boat around the tongues of glaciers that in some places extended to the sea. They already had a

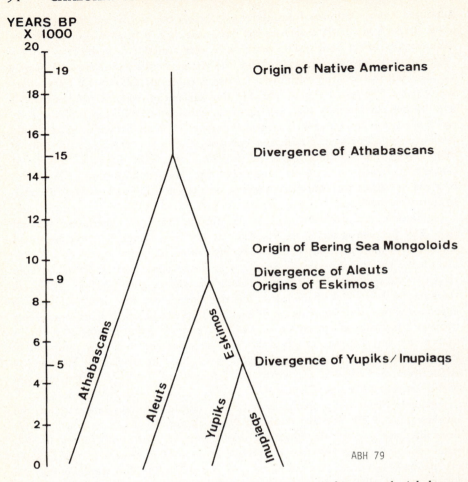

Fig. 39. Using the same genetic evidence for Aleuts, Eskimos, and Athabascan Indians, and allowing 9000 years for the divergence of Aleuts from Bering Sea Mongoloids, the Indians broke off earlier, probably in Siberia. The Eskimos originated when the Aleuts diverged, and the two major divisions of Eskimos (Yupik and Inupiaq) separated approximately 5000 years ago (courtesy A. B. Harper).

complex culture and they were well prepared to exploit the coastline, although we do not know if they had both the open *baidar* and the decked *baidarka*. They had to adjust their living sites to rising sea levels. Most of the older sites—older than 9000 years—are probably underwater. Chaluka was founded after the establishment of the modern sea level, and the Aleuts should be able to remain there for another 4000 years.

Drawing upon the data presented in Chapters 2, 6, 7, and 9, it is now possible to assign a date to the origins and divergence system of the Indians, Aleuts, and Eskimos. Dr. A. B. Harper has formulated the degree of genetic similarity between these three major Alaskan populations, and has scaled the time component using 9000 years, based on the Nikolski Bay occupation by ancestral Aleuts (Harper, 1979). His time and divergence model (Fig. 39) is in excellent agreement with the linguistic divergence (Krauss, 1974, 1979), and with the archeological evidence. The long history of the Aleuts has thus contributed to the first measured time scale of human evolution for the entire human species.

8 / The use and abuse of mummies

In the eastern and central Aleutians, the Aleuts frequently made mummies of some of their dead people and stored these mortuary packages in caves or in rock shelters. Along with the mummies they often included the kayaks and hunting equipment of the men, armor, shields, knives, drums, masks, and with the women various dishes of wood, knives, basketry, mats, and other utensils. All in all, these mummy caves are actually museums showing much of the material culture of the people and of the people themselves, for their skeletons and much of their bodies are preserved; at the same time they reflect much of the religious beliefs. The Kagamil mummies, numbering about 234 in all, constitute an excellent demographic sample of the Kagamil community. It includes persons of both sexes and of all ages (Fig. 40).

The manufacture of mummies indicated as much technical skill as the manufacture of boats. Many items of the material culture, especially those made of perishable materials such as basketry, wood, and skins or sinew, could not be recovered from excavations in the village mounds because they had decayed in the earth. Only the mummy caves and the collections made by early European visitors showed the range of things made by the people, in addition to the skill and artistry with which they made them.

The preparation of a mummy presupposes an interest and competence in anatomy as well as a reason for wanting to preserve the dead and, therefore, no simple fear of the dead. Mummification was not an isolated achievement or bizarre trait but an understandable practice firmly rooted in a pragmatically oriented culture. The facts that the Aleuts studied comparative anatomy, using the sea otter as the form most similar to man, and that they conducted autopsies upon people who died, are closely related. Their knowledge of human anatomy is amply demonstrated in their enormous vocabulary for anatomical terms. The basic objective was the preservation and use of the spiritual power that resided in the human body. This power could be retained in the body or let out of the body, but in all cases, it had to be regulated and handled with expert care.

There are three customs that shed light upon each other and upon the reasons for making mummies: first, the actual manufacture of mummies, including their uses; second, the practice of dismemberment of certain people, hawks, and owls; and third, the custom of binding the joints of pubescent girls, widows, and widowers. Taken as a whole, these practices and their underlying beliefs form a

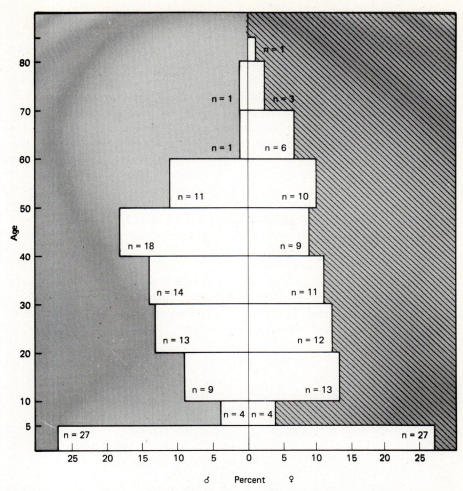

Fig. 40. Age at death of Kagamil mummies. Total number = 194 (as of Feb. 28, 1979) based on crania and reasonably complete skeletons and excluding dissociated long bones and 12 of the intact child and adult mummy bundles. Male number = 64, female number = 62, plus 68 unsexed children divided equally between the sexes.

major nucleus of Aleut culture and supply the meaning for what would otherwise remain only lovely art objects and skillful manufactures.

MUMMIFICATION

The body of a deceased person was kept inside the house where he died, sometimes for several months. Often, but not always, the viscera were removed. Most often an incision was made in the lower abdomen and the intestines were drawn out through it. Other organs might also be removed at the same time. Dried grass was then stuffed into the abdominal cavity. The body was carefully and frequently wiped and, of course, kept quite dry. Without exception, the body was flexed, with the knees drawn up to the chin, the heels against the rump and the arms drawn or folded so that the hands were frequently covering the face. A common way of handling the body was to place it in a large cradle of the same sort used for infants. This cradle was made with a wood frame, round or rectangular with rounded corners, and a leather basin deeper on one side than the other. It could be carried on a mother's back or suspended from a beam when inside the house. For the deceased, the cradle was suspended from a roof beam over the same place that the person ordinarily slept. Finally, the relatives would dress the contracted body in its best garments and encase it in various layers of seal or sea lion skins and perhaps a layer of mats or of basketry. The entire bundle was finally lashed with braided sinew cord. In at least one case, nets had been used for the final lashing (Fig. 41). It might then be set in a wooden dish or in a cradle for removal to a cave and its final position. It is likely that the mummy was ready for removal by the thirty-first day after death but, owing to wishes of surviving relatives, was sometimes kept in the house much longer.

If a somewhat secluded cave or rock overhang was nearby, within a kilometer, the mummy might be carried there. The essential prerequisite was to keep the mummy dry, although close to the ocean. These *asxinan* (departed ones), sometimes called "the dry ones," carried on a full round of activities at night, including

Fig. 41. Kagamil Aleut mummy bundle unopened. It was found suspended in a cave. The different mesh sizes of nets used for shroud wrapping illustrates the diversity of pre-Russian sinew nets.

hunting, eating, and dancing. Therefore the activities needed to be held near the ocean. Inside the caves, the mummies were placed on hewn planks supported by scaffolding. The posts had to be driven into cracks in the stone or wedged tightly between top and bottom because there was not enough earth to set posts in the ground. On Carlisle Island, we found portions of mummies that had fallen to the shore some 70 feet (21.4 meters) below when the cave itself had been destroyed by wave action cutting into the cliff. Remnants of the ends of posts were still wedged in place in the inner wall.

A number of mummies, over 35, had been placed in a rock shelter or overhanging cliff on Ship Rock, a small island in the pass between Umnak Island and Unalaska Island. Apparently they were placed on the ground (rocks) and planks were laid over them, with the upper ends of the planks resting against the cliff wall. They and some whalebone also used for the facing had been painted red. Still another type of burial was in a rectangular log tomb, divided into compartments. Such a burial ground was found on top of Split Rock near Kashega, Unalaska Island.

More commonly, if no cave or rock shelter were available, a little wood and sod hut was constructed for the purpose. Timbers, roughly the size of fenceposts, were stacked against each other, forming a little conical tent. Over them, sod was placed. The grass on the sod continued to grow and eventually the little house blended into the color of the countryside, but could be distinguished by its shape. We found such a burial hut (*ulakan*) on Kanaga Island in 1938. The contracted skeleton of a robust male lay on the floor, although it may originally have been suspended from the top.

Equally common was the burial of people in the debris surrounding the houses and found underneath them. These are the ones found in the excavations of the old village sites. In some cases, a house was abandoned and the dead were left sitting on a mat. Figure 42 shows such a mat. An old lady in Nikolski made this for me, when I pointed out that I needed one to die on. She made it small because she did not have enough dried grass for a large one and anyway I did not need to die for a while. It is a death mat in the sense that a man would have a fine mat of this kind for ceremonial occasions and would be wrapped in it after he died. The name for this mat is *luuk*, and is a general word for similar mats.

Occasionally, a hunter was mummified and placed in his kayak, harpoon in hand, ready to resume the hunt. We found some beautifully made kayak frames in the warm cave on Kagamil Island. Well over 50 mummies were taken from this cave.

Most mummies have been found in the eastern Aleutians, some in the central area (Amlia, Ilak, Kanaga, and Tanaga), but none have been reported for Attu or other of the Near Island group in the west. According to one Aleut, the Attu people did not "believe in mummies." It is likely that this custom was diffusing from east to west and had not yet reached the more remote islands before the arrival of the Russians interfered with its cultural transfer. The most famous caves are the two on the southwest coast of Kagamil Island in the Islands of Four Mountains group, just 26 miles (42 kilometers) west of Nikolski. Although the stories about these two caves were common knowledge to the Russians and to early American traders, it was not until 1874 that Captain E. Hennig of the Alaska Com-

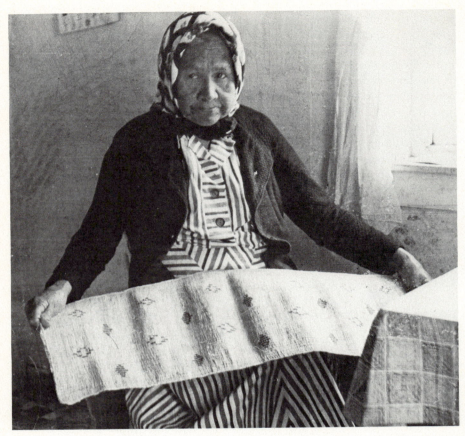

Fig. 42. Nikolski, 1950. Mrs. Heratina Sovoroff holds a woven grass death mat. Many kinds of matting were woven. This kind was used as a sleeping mat and for wrapping a dead person. The one illustrated here was made small because the weaver did not want the recipient of this gift to die soon.

mercial Company was able to locate the caves and to land some hunters there in good weather. He removed 12 mummies and saw that they were sent to museums for safe keeping and study. Dr. Hrdlička entered the caves in 1936:

> Secured in all over 50 mummies, though mostly children; and about 30 separate skulls, besides many loose bones. In addition, a great quantity of remarkably made and decorated matting, some damaged, but some still good, and a mass of shreds of fur (sea otter) and feather garments, feathers of dried-up birds, dried bird wings, shreds of ingeniously made cords, many pieces of worked wood from kayaks, or armor, etc. (Hrdlička, 1945, pp. 242–243).

This cave, the more northerly of the pair, was quite warm and a large steam fumerole some 100 yards in front of the cave sent an expanding jet of steam over 60 feet (18.3 meters) into the air. The shoreline here consists of giant boulders and below them percolating hot springs maintain a constant susurration in the sulphurous water. In 1938 the debris in the bottom of the cave was so warm that it was uncomfortable to the bare hand; by 1948 it had cooled considerably. One Umnak story describes a contest between the Kagamil people who steamed their food and the Carlisle people who boiled their food. They settled the issue by a *baidar* race from Kagamil to Umnak. The Carlisle people won the race and since then boiled food has been considered better than steamed food.

A short distance south of the warm cave lies the cold or wet cave entered by Hrdlička in 1936. Its floor and ceiling are wet and everything that is exposed is extremely damp. The contents were not as well preserved, although both caves had suffered from foxes who lived and ate in the caves. More recently vandals and robbers have looted these vaults of remaining items. The floor of this wet cave was littered with skulls, bones, and a wealth of artifacts, but only one mummy was in a good state of preservation. Many were still flexed and articulated, but their wrappings, muscles, and some of their bones had been gnawed by foxes. Hrdlička noted on the original visit that there had been several tiers of mummies laid on scaffolding and planks that had collapsed.

The antiquity of these caves is probably only a few hundred years at most. The Nikolski Aleuts still had much information about the caves and appeared familiar with some of the persons interred there. They repeated a traditional story that places the first of these burials in the winter of the same year in which the Aleuts saw the first Russians who arrived the following spring. Another estimate places them between 1720 and 1730. Canvas, glass beads, and a possible case of syphilis on one of the skeletons indicate the continued use of these caves after Russian arrival, and actual use is well attested in various historical accounts.

The story of the earliest use of the warm cave, intended to explain the beginning of the practice of mummification in the Islands of Four Mountains and possibly for the Aleuts in general, involves a rich and distinguished headman, named Little Wren, of the village on top of the island, Kagam-Ilan, just south of the cave. He built a little kayak (*iqyak*) for his 13- or 14-year-old son and saw him safely launched into the sea with the admonition to stay close to shore. The boy, however, started hunting a diving bird that led him out to sea. He was seen by his brother-in-law from a nearby island, who was coming over to visit his pregnant wife, the boy's sister. The brother-in-law admired the skill of the young lad and then threw a small harpoon near the boy to startle him. By accident he hit the boy, who then capsized and drowned before the brother-in-law could rescue him. He towed the boy to shore and left him in the kelp where his father found him the following morning. Having convened all the people of the Islands of Four Mountains for the funeral, they proceeded to the old burial place. On the way the boy's pregnant sister stepped on a stone lying across the path and slipped, thus killing herself and her unborn child. The season was late, snowy, and cold so the father decided to place the bodies in the cave that had previously been used as a storage cache. After the ceremonies, which included lamentations, singing, beating drums, and interment of the bodies with many possessions, he announced his intention to make a mausoleum of this cave for his entire family and that he himself should be placed there when he died. Little Wren soon died of grief and was placed there with all his wealth—sea otter and fur seal skins, household utensils, wooden dishes, and hunting equipment. The Nikolski Aleuts mentioned that the headman was named Little Wren because he was a small man and was therefore named after a small bird. They also thought that one of the mummies recovered by Captain Hennig in 1874 was that of Little Wren.

Beliefs about mummy caves are best illustrated with an actual account. In 1925, three men from Nikolski were trapping blue fox on Ilak Island. Although it was winter, one of the men noticed that the grass was very green in one place on the side of the hill at the west end of this small granite island. He climbed up from the shore and then noticed mummies inside the cave below the green area. Like the Ship Rock mummies, these were placed behind planks that leaned against the side of the cave. He immediately climbed back down without entering the cave and bathed himself in the sea using a special medicinal plant. He advised his partner to wash himself in the same way but his partner said he did not believe in that. However, two days after returning to Nikolski, the unwashed member of the partnership broke out in a red rash over his entire body. The oldest member of the party learned of this and told him to wash himself with the plant as the other had done. He washed, took a steam bath, and was completely free of the rash on the following day. When the wife of one of the men walked by the cave entrance, although she remained on the shore, the cave entrance turned red, as all mummy caves are supposed to do when improperly visited.

As recently as 1862, the advice of mummies was sought. The Russian Orthodox priest Lavrenty Salamatov of Atka encountered the continuing belief in the power of mummies. He noted, in his travel journal, that during paganism the Aleuts made mummies that they called "dry ones" or *askhanas* ("dead"), by removing the viscera, clothing the body, and placing it with the deceased person's possessions in a lying or, more often, in a sitting position inside a dry cave. The Aleuts then paid the same homage to these mummies as to their idols. To learn about the success of a hunting expedition, a man would prepare himself by fasting, by avoiding his wife, by washing in a stream and by dressing in his best clothes. Cleansed, inside and out, he approached the mummy cave and called out in a loud voice, "I am coming to you to find out about ————. Show me what is to be." He then carried a gift into the cave and placed it before the mummy. The gift might be black paint or ochre and the wing or feather of a hawk. He then withdrew for a while. During the hunter's absence the "dry one" displayed various objects that were interpreted as a sign for the future.

Salamatov, who had himself seen some mummies on Atka and Amlia Islands, cites a particular case showing the persistence of beliefs in the prophetic powers of mummies. A hunting party of Amlia Aleuts from an island adjacent to Atka had been fox hunting on Kanaga Island. Some of them went into a cave to find out about their future. Finding seals' hair in the cave, they inferred that they would have a successful seal hunt before returning home to Atka. On their way to Ulak to hunt seals, all 13 men were drowned.

Whaling with "a-piece-of-dead-man" illustrates an interesting ritual in addition to the object inserted into the whale. A finger joint or grease from a mummy of a great whaler was a powerful charm for the living hunter. However, they did not use this ultimate weapon for killing the whale, or else all the people who ate the whale would die. The top whaler, *alananasiska*, or the one who had killed a few whales, *alanaxnax*, might carry a finger joint or some piece of a mummy for the power it gave them. They did not, however, insert it into the whale. Mummy grease smeared upon ivory would prevent it from eroding, thus exerting a beneficent power. However, those who used such strong power died prematurely.

DISMEMBERMENT

Dismemberment of a slain enemy or dangerous person was a regular and necessary way of protecting the living survivor from a fatal encounter. The practice was applied to honored birds, such as the hawk and owl, whose feathers were used for ceremonial and magical purposes. The reason for dismembering enemies was held to be so obvious and necessary that it was first overlooked. One evening in Nikolski an Aleut lady was telling me of her father's encounter with an "outside man." Outside men (*ashadan*) were considered renegades or marauders, or simply rugged individualists, who chose to live alone or in the company of similar men away from the villages. Mothers employ accounts of them as a bugaboo to prevent their children from wandering away from the villages, and effectively succeed in frightening themselves in the process. This lady's father, Iliodor Sokolnikof, was building a kayak frame on a shingle stone beach some two miles north of Nikolski. He laid his hatchet down on the stones while he walked up the beach to find some more wood. Going over a rocky outcrop that interrupted the beach, he looked up and saw an outside man standing there, looking out to sea. He recognized the man as an outside man by the appearance of his clothes. They were made of seal skins but not in the neat fashion of that made by a seamstress. He turned and ran back with the outside man following in hot pursuit. He was overtaken at the place where he had been making his kayak and a fierce struggle ensued. The outside man finally bested him, throwing him to the ground and leaping on top of him. Just as Iliodor felt he was about to be killed, his hand touched the hatchet he had laid there. Seizing this, he staged a timely comeback, repulsing and killing his assailant. Having done this, he proceeded to chop the outside man apart, cutting off the arms and legs of the body and cutting them apart at the joints. He then threw the disarticulated parts into the sea. Parts of the deceased were later recovered and buried in the ground. Investigation revealed that Mr. Sokolnikof had not dismembered his attacker in a frenzy of anger, although he may not have been in his best humor at the end of the contest. Rather, he was doing what must be done to preserve his own health from the power that would have remained in the body of the man he killed if he had not let it out.

Other actual accounts tallied with this one, and the reasoning was in each case the same. The enemy continued to be dangerous as long as his body remained intact. A young Aleut girl, shortly before the turn of the century, was digging orchid roots on the Pacific side of Umnak, some three miles from Nikolski on the east side of Driftwood Bay. An outside man lay hiding in the deep grass and when she was close to him he seized her. Fortunately, she had an excellent weapon in her hand, a solid whalebone root-digger, and she proceeded to whack him over the head with it. She managed to kill him and immediately ran back to Nikolski in great fright. Unfortunately, she did not pause to dismember him. In consequence of this oversight, she suffered in later years from severe inflammation of the joints.

Many examples of dismemberment occur in the legendary and historical stories of the Aleuts. Some of the early Russian accounts of fighting with the Aleuts refer to the horrible mutilation practiced upon the dead Russians by the Aleuts. The Aleuts were of course proceeding in standard fashion; the only way to keep a strong man down is to kill him and then disassemble him. Dismemberment is not confined to the Aleutians but appears frequently in the Eskimo world also.

JOINT-BINDING

Just as mummification preserves the power in the body and dismemberment lets it out, so joint-binding regulates the power in the body during crucial periods in the life of the individual. Joint-binding is practiced when a young girl has her first menstrual period, and when a husband or wife dies. The custom survived over a century after Veniaminov's description. When a young girl found that she was beginning her menses, she informed an old woman, often a village midwife. Under the direction of the old woman, she began a 40-day period of confinement in a dark room (formerly a separate hut). In addition to the 40-day period, 10 more days were added in which she could go on a special walk but still could not have visitors nor look at the sky. Also, an ensuing five-month period was imposed during which she could not travel on the sea or cross over a salmon stream.

Each joint of the girl, ankle, knee, wrist, elbow, and shoulder, was bound. String from a flour sack could be used if it was waxed. In addition to these bindings, a special sewn cloth belt was worn, the neck was bound, and the hair was tied in one braid at the back of the head. The hair was secured with gut (intestine) that had been bleached white. In the words of an old and skilled midwife, "The strings are tied on the joints so they won't ache or get crooked when they get old."

Every five days the girl took a bath in which she was doused with a small amount of water and scrubbed with a plant (*cimxuux*) instead of soap—the same plant used for washing after seeing a mummy cave. Several food restrictions were imposed on the girl and whatever food she could have was eaten in small amounts. She could not eat the head or tail of a fish; otherwise she would be like a fish and would have bad manners. During the 40-day period the girl could wash her own clothes but could not hang them on a line. Rather, she must lay them on the ground to dry. If they were hung in the wind, then all the animals and ducks that are hunted would not come around. She could not use her fingernails to scratch herself but must use a little back-scratcher.

Along with the things the girl could not do, there were many that she could and should do. She should be busy with sewing and weaving baskets. If her stitches were not just right, they had to be done over. This was a period of learning and she would do things in the future the same way she did them during this confinement. She could not touch anything that a man would use, but she might make a miniature *kamleika* or boots for practice. The potentially curative aspects of the power in the girl's body, a power that could be intensified at critical periods, were used at this time as well as later.

Like all other people, Aleuts might suffer from seasickness, but this disability was considerably more serious among men who had to make their living on the sea. A boy or man who suffered from this debility could bring food to the girl, which she warmed in her hands and fed to him. For various pains, she chewed her tongue and then rubbed the spittle over the ailing part such as a sore back, a stiff elbow, or even sores on the body. She could not, however, treat an open wound or cut. She might give a small bit of grass from her bed to a man "who doesn't want the breakers to get him wet," or to prevent swamping when he is out in his dory.

The belt or girdle holds special powers. After the 40-day period is over, this belt might be coiled up and applied to the ailing part of anyone who made the necessary arrangements for its use. During confinement the girl could weave a special inside belt or "charm belt" that was braided of sinew or string. A man could carry this belt as a charm against a variety of hazards.

The treatment of a widow or widower was similar to that of the young girl. In the case of a man, he must not go outside his house. If a woman, she must not sew on anything used by a man. Gloves were worn, as they might also be worn by a young girl. A significant difference appears in the case of a surviving widow. Her joints were bound three days after the man was buried, and her 40-day isolation began at the same time. Counting the day of the death, this is four days, the usual repetitive ritual number associated with men, contrasted to five for women. On the thirtieth day, she received an additional set of bindings. The cuffs and throat of her dress were bound with bindings like those inside on the skin. This thirtieth day binding is "for the dead man." After he has been buried 30 days his bones come apart.

The belt worn by the widow is enormously powerful, far more than that of the young girl enduring her first confinement. The widow kept her "strong belt" which she could loan out when someone asked for it. Like all valuable things, it had to be kept dry and clean, so it was wrapped in gut. If it should be lost and thus not buried with her when she died and was later found, it would then be burned. After 40 days the widow could marry again, unless she had children, in which case she must continue her confinement for an additional 10 days.

The belt worn by a pregnant woman in delivering her baby was not useful for curing purposes. It appears that the belt worn by the girl menstruating for the first time and by the widow derived their curative powers from the body at the two times when they had been used to regulate and retain the power in their bodies.

BRINGING IN THE WHALE

The concern and seriousness of joint-binding and dismemberment, and the fear that, if not properly done, the participants would be visited by arthritis or joint diseases, did not prevent the basic humor of the Aleuts from poking through along with some elements of pride. If a man were a successful hunter and always returned safely, the woman who cured him of seasickness or who had given him a powerful charm could claim much credit. A particularly charming account of female accomplishment concerns the beaching of a whale by a young girl, later an aged and distinguished lady who had helped many people with her medical treatments when she recounted her achievement. She was justifiably proud of the fact that she had been of substantial benefit to the village when she was only 19 years old. At that time, she was living at Chungsun on the Pacific side of Umnak. She was confined to the house because of her monthly period, a confinement of five days during which she ceased to carry on household activities and avoided contact with men and with anything connected with hunting or fishing. A large dead whale (*chikagluux*—California gray whale) came drifting toward the shore. She was told not to watch the whale, but her curiosity overcame her regard for the rules and she peeked. As a consequence, the whale did not drift in easily and the men had much difficulty getting it on the shore. When the men found that she had been looking, and therefore repulsing the whale, they brought her out of the house and sent her around the whale so that she could repulse it from the seaward side, thus pushing it firmly ashore. Since there was deep water on the seaward side of this wayward whale, the men built a raft and floated her around it. She took great pleasure the rest of her life in what she had done with her power. Few men could tell, let alone verify, a fish story of these dimensions.

9 / Words, language, and culture

The Aleut language is complex and superbly expressive, and it accommodates beautifully to the entire range of human thought. Major cultural interests are easily recognizable in the vocabulary and in the structure. Among these are the concern with relationships, with the marine environment, and with human anatomy. Interestingly, the language elaborated a counting system so that it was simple for Aleuts to reckon into tens of thousands, unlike their Koniag neighbors who succeeded in counting only to 200 and then proceeded with difficulty.

The language can be described formally by its structural characteristics: three basic vowel positions; 14 consonants; the extensive use of suffixes (there are no prefixes); the presence of a dual ending; lack of stress on long vowels; an absence of most bilabials in the Eastern dialect; and many other diagnostic linguistic features.

It can be also characterized as an observer's language, ideal for describing things as they are, for explaining their relations to each other, and for distinguishing between direct and indirect evidence. For events or things that the discussant describes but does not actually witness with his own eyes, a formal distinction is made so that the listener or reader knows what things were actually witnessed and what things were inferred or were hearsay. This aspect of the language is probably one of the reasons why Aleuts are reliable and accurate witnesses, informally as well as in court. An informant may point out that he does not know, or that he is uncertain and recommend another source of more accurate information in response to a question. When an Aleut says "I don't know," he may actually know a great deal but only from hearsay or circumstantial information. His ingrained regard for facts, secured as an eyewitness or by participation, may lead him to remark that he does not know.

The basic sounds of Aleut are quite similar to English and to Russian. Aleuts do not speak in guttural tones down low in the throat. Rather, the uvular stop represented by *q*, as in *umqan*, a place used for burials, is as far down as they go. The *s* is a more apical or broader *s* than English, and the sound *d* is a little more like *th* than the English *d*. The vowels may be front or back in position, and long or short. Long vowels are critically important in Aleut and they do not automatically carry the accent as they do in English, as for example in *saloon* or *lagoon*, in *reprieve* or *conceive*. Unalaska, a major village and island, is pronounced without accent on the vowels in spite of their length. Epenthetic vowels or glide sounds are often inserted between consonants in the spoken but not in the written form. Thus the word for "blood" is *amgigh* (the *gh* ending is not voiced) but the word is pronounced with an *a* between the *m* and *g*, *am(a)gigh*. Such an inserted vowel does not alter the meaning of the word and is, therefore, not considered to have phonemic value. In order to read Aleut, it is necessary to hear it spoken, a similarity shared with English.

The early introduction of Russian loan words induced pronunciations that survived in some cases and disappeared in others. Since eastern Aleut had no bilabials (*p, b, f, v*) and no *r*, other sounds had to be substituted. The Siberian Russian word for an underground house, *barabara*, therefore was handled with *m* substituted for *b*, and *l* for *r*, and the word, *malamala* was the workable result. The Russian word for "pump" became the Aleut word *muma* with the second *m* nasalized and voiceless. A variant form was *munma*. Correspondences between Eskimo and Aleut words can be identified in some cases where the Eskimo word has a bilabial and the Aleut word employs an *m*. An Eskimo word for blood, *avik*, corresponds to an old Aleut form *am(a)gh*, and an Eskimo word for knife, *saviq*, is similar to an old Aleut word *samagh*.

Because of the broad nature of the Aleut *s*, the loan word for "shop" could be written with only three letters, *cap*, using the Aleut *s* and the Russian *p*. The result sounds like English *shop*. Tobacco was simply converted to *tamaka*. Some Russian words have come into current use with little or no alteration. The Aleuts took over the Siberian Russian word *baidar* for their large, open skin boat (the Eskimo *umiak*), and then indicated the smaller covered boat (Eskimo *kayak*) with a diminutive ending, *baidarka*. This is pronounced as "baidarky" and is often written with a terminal *y*. In this case, the Aleuts followed the relationship indicated in their word for the single-hatch decked boat, which has the stem for the large open boat with a diminutive added to indicate that it is smaller. The new Russian word *baidarka* could also be applied to the two-hatch and to the three-hatch covered boats. In Aleut, these are different words.

Loan words are also subject to metathesis, the transposition of letters or sounds within a word. The Aleuts refer to pictures as *patritan*, reversing the *rt* from the Russian word *portret*. Most of the loan words simply have an Aleut ending added. Sometimes old or relatively unused Russian words have survived in Aleut. Thus the Aleut word for an outhouse is based on the term used on Russian sailing ships.

Aleut is technically known as a polysynthetic language because an infinite number of ideas can be joined together in one word. By adding endings (suffixes),, a large number of ideas can be expressed in a single word. The word may be very long, however, and the order of meaningful items must follow a complex series of rules. Aleut and Eskimo are the only languages in the world that have only suffixes and no prefixes. All the modifiers are at the end, following the stem word. The longest word in Aleut is written with 35 characters, a good deal longer than any word in English. This was pointed out to me (in fact, was written out) by an Aleut who enjoyed working with words, riddles, double meanings, and related Aleut pastimes.

Bilabial sounds, common in English and in Russian, may be difficult for some Aleut speakers because they are generally lacking in Aleut—with notable exceptions in the central and western dialects. (See Fig. 43 for the distribution of the three Aleut dialects.) This group includes our sound *w*. One evening, while working

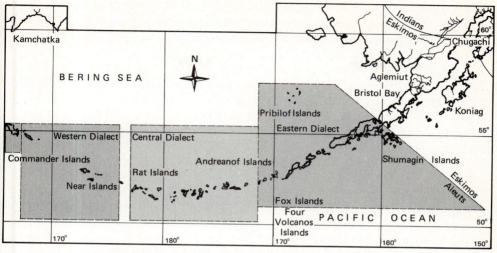

Fig. 43. Map showing distribution of the three Aleut dialects.

over a list of birds seen by an Aleut (106 species) we came to ruin on the pigeon and the widgeon. Only with the aid of pictures were we able to find out which bird we were discussing. Even today in a little used word such as *sword* the *w* may be pronounced.

It is of interest to know whether bilingualism helps, hinders, or has no effect on learning the two languages and on the Aleut perception of the sounds of speech. The best evidence indicates that the differences in sounds between the two languages do not hinder recognition of the recurrent consonants in English (*b, d, g, k, p, v*) when presented in a dichotic listening test in which different sounds are presented to each ear simultaneously. The Aleuts perform like other Americans and those who are involved in a bilingual program do better than those who are not (Milman, 1973). A program in bilingual instruction in Atka, in which the Norwegian linguist Knud Bergsland served as the preceptor with five Atka Aleuts has been eminently successful in promoting "good" Aleut as well as "good" English and in encouraging those persons with the interest and skill to prepare written materials in Aleut.

It is difficult to describe Aleut in the traditional categories employed for European languages, such as nouns, verbs, adjectives, tenses, and conjugations. They are not always applicable and a literal translation of an Aleut story may appear to be quaint or disorderly when, in fact, it carries more carefully specified meaning than an English story of equivalent length. Strictly speaking, there are no tenses in Aleut. When things took place or take place is indicated in a relative manner. Aleut can express sequence with precision. Aleut can, of course, be forced into European categories, but then it ceases to be Aleut.

WORDS

The Aleuts enjoyed a rich material culture. They made many kinds of things of wood, grass, animal tissues, bone, ivory, and stone. Therefore, there is much information locked into the names of material objects, and these names or terms often give some evidence of the form, function, use, or meaning of these artifacts. They reveal something of the system of categorization and the psychology of the Aleuts.

A set of bolas is a device consisting of some 8 to 16 small stones or pieces of ivory joined together by sinew cords to each weight. The stem of the name for this hunting device, *aka*, means "up." The name of the weapon means "that which is thrown up" and agrees with the use of this device. An Aleut who had used the bolas pointed out some of the spots about Umnak Lake where the hunters lay in the deep grass, waiting for ducks to fly down onto the lake or up from the lake. The hunters lay concealed in the grass and then threw the bolas up into the ducks to entangle them as they passed close overhead.

An example of meaning contained in the name of an object is that of *kaathaagaa-thagh*, the image of the deity. This is a small figure, usually less than six inches in height, made of stone, bone, or ivory. These are known only from excavated specimens. A key feature is the vertical girdle about the head by which they were suspended from a ceiling beam in the house. The hunter spoke to the image before venturing out on the ocean and the image spoke back with useful information about weather and the hunt. Some of these figures were carved in a skeletonized form and some had holes in which offerings were inserted. In post-Russian times a little tobacco might be given the figure. The diminutive ending *aathaagh* indicates that this is a small image of the real or larger deity who resides elsewhere.

The image of the deity is a key trait in Aleut culture. A specimen has been recovered from the floor of an old house in Chaluka (4000 years ago; see Fig. 44), and a number have been retrieved from successively younger strata, continuing on into the post-Russian period. The name explains the meaning. The girdles about the head indicate the use, and the form indicates the Mongoloid racial affinity of the Aleuts (see photographs of specimen and of modern Aleut). In addition, the object reflects an art style. However, to designate such a figure as simply an art object would deprive it of its meaning.

The name for the single-piece socket of whalebone into which the harpoon head was inserted is informative of its shape and of its history. The socket piece is bifurcated into two projecting prongs which articulate with the wood shaft of the harpoon. Those prongs, of course, are "its two feet," and a dual ending fits nicely. Furthermore, using archeological evidence, it appears that the predecessor of this single-piece socket was a two-piece socket, and the dual ending of the name probably persists from the earlier form of the object.

The name for a grass mat and for the sail used on the *baidar* is the same. Prior to the use of canvas sails, the Aleuts had devised their own finely woven grass mat sails. Grass weaving was developed to a fine art form by Aleuts who not only produced the tightly woven "Attu" basketry, but also grass socks, pellerines (based on the Russian model of the shoulder robe), and specialized ceremonial figures as well.

The term for flaking a stone arrow or harpoon head point uses the same stem as the word for the palm of the hand and confirms the basic method of chipping stone tools by holding the piece to be chipped in the palm of one hand. The name for the halibut hook, *kuuluusagh*, is the Aleut name for the Tlingit, the Indians of

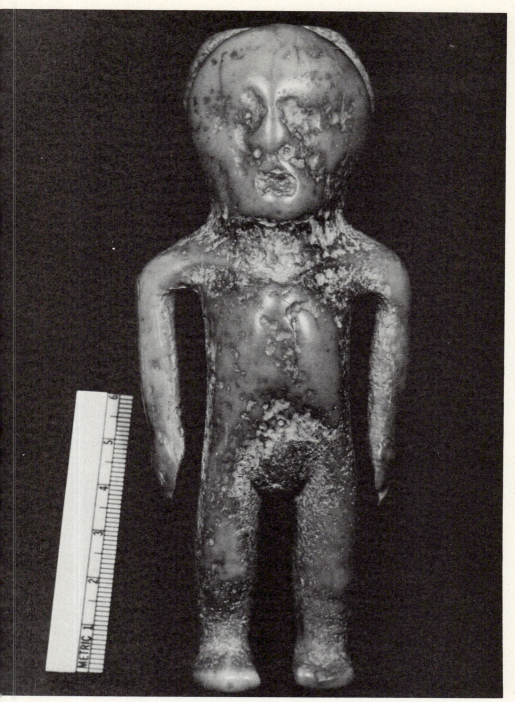

Fig. 44. Image of the deity, kaathaagaathagh, 1948. A key feature of this ivory figure is the girdle about the head for suspension from a house beam. Though no longer used, they have been treated respectfully up to the present.

southern Alaska whose older name is still preserved in the name for a linguistic stock, *Kolosh*, the name most commonly used for them by the Russians. This kind of fishhook has been diffused from the Indians of the North Pacific coast through the Eskimos to the Aleuts.

Place names often described the shape of the geographic feature and were intended to be informative. A single bay had several names for its different parts and outstanding features, so that an Aleut could say where he was going or where he had been with precision. The European habit of inflicting personal names on geographic features was seldom if ever practiced, for it would have been highly disruptive to travel and hunting.

Cape Chagak is located on the northwest coast of Umnak Island. Inland and up on the slopes of Okmok Crater is an exposed lens of obsidian, a volcanic glass used for chipped stone points and scrapers. The Aleut word for "obsidian" is *chagak* and indicates that this was the source of obsidian. It is in fact the only known source of obsidian for the Aleutian Islands and Alaska Peninsula.

Another kind of analysis can be applied to place names that reveals a more subtly expressed conception of a geographic form. Anangula Island, discussed in Chapter 3, cannot be analyzed into components that provide any more meaning, but the names for the parts of the island do reveal how it was seen by the Aleuts. Seen from the waterline, this island gives the appearance of an animal swimming north through the sea with just its head, back, and long, tapering tail protruding. It is clear that the Aleuts envisaged it as a whale, without explicitly stating the resemblance. Their name for the northeast end of the island means "the bust of Anangula," using as the word for "bust," a term that designates the head and shoulders of a sea mammal—*qiganga*—but does not specify which sea mammal. The long, low southwestern tail is termed "the tail of Anangula"—*Anaguulam chmagh*—with their term for "tail," which can apply only to the tail of a whale or of a fish, but not for any other mammal. After we assemble these two pieces of information, we see that the sea mammal indicated is a whale.

The name of Anangula Island provides information on linguistic change and may indicate a westward movement in dialect. The designation of the island on United States Coast and Geodetic Survey charts is Ananiuliak, a transliteration of the Russianized form *Ananyulyakh* of the original Aleut name *Anangulagh*, from which we have subtracted the unvoiced ending *gh* to give Anangula. The change in the Aleut form of the name from *Anangulagh* to *Anagulagh* took place after the arrival of the Russians on Umnak Island. It is possible that the central dialect was spoken in this area at that time, but that cannot be demonstrated from existing evidence. The Aleut language was constantly changing, like any other language. Fortunately, many Aleut names were preserved on Russian charts and, therefore, the changes that subsequently took place can be studied. Amak Island, north of Cold Bay on the Alaska Peninsula, is the old Aleut word for "walrus." The more recent word for "walrus" is *amagadagh*. The Americans copied the Russian charts without consulting the Aleuts about their name for their island and thereby inadvertently preserved a useful piece of linguistic information. Walrus skeletons are still found on Amak Island, although few walrus drift this far west. The paucity of walrus along the peninsula is partly a function of excessive early commercial hunting of walrus for their ivory tusks.

Names of persons are also informative. They may describe characteristic activities as well as personal idiosyncrasies. The names of the two Umnak Aleuts who led the successful 1764 uprising against the Medvedev Cossacks were "Old-Wornout-Stomach," and "Kills-Lots-of-Ducks." The stomach referred to the stomach of a seal or sea lion used for storage of dried salmon or oil. "Kills-Many-Ducks" was obviously a successful hunter and his name reminds us that birds were very important in the Aleut diet. The great-grandfather of a Nikolski Aleut was named "One-Who-Suns-Himself," a man who liked to bask in the sun. Unless the weather was much better in the early eighteenth century, the prevailing fog and cloud cover did not permit him to indulge himself very often. This man lived at the south end of Umnak and stored some whale meat in an underground pit before leaving for three years of sea otter hunting for the Russians. When he returned, the meat was still good. "Always-Kills-Many-on-the-Mainland" indicates the honor attached to killing Eskimos and his apparent skill. "Little Killer Whale," "Little Wren," "Little Guillemot," "Small Knife"—all employ a diminutive ending. Diminutives appended to a name indicate endearment in Aleut.

The opposite expression of dislike interestingly employs an augmentative. The name for a wooden face mask, such as those worn in dances, also has an augmentative ending. Such masks were ritually important and treated with great care. Thus an Aleut who was disgusted with his pet dog referred to it as a "big" old dog. "Ivory-Breaker-Up" refers to a strong man who could smash ivory tusks of the walrus. The same man is the one credited with traveling from Tigalda to St. Paul Island in the Pribilof Islands, thus preceding the Russian discovery of these rich islands. "Soup-Ladle" is a rather worthless man in the story in which he is described and corresponds to a kind of pan-handler. "Looks-Like-Copper," "Man-With-One-Eye," and "Hard Rock" are evidently descriptive of appearance and possibly durability in the latter.

A full range of personalities can be secured from names of women. Thus "Summer-Face-Woman" was a kind of Lorelei, and "Teeth Woman" was a fictitious child who became a monster. She finally ate all the men of a village except her own brother, who was spared by the happy accident of wandering away while she was following her cannibalistic bent.

The use of true Aleut names, often animals and birds, continues in diminished form today. They are not ordinarily used in front of outsiders and they may be misinterpreted as nicknames. Names applied to outsiders are rarely or never used in their presence, as a matter of politeness and in recognition of the outsider's probable lack of a sense of humor. The large and obese schoolteacher named "Sea Lion" might have been discomfited if she had known her name and what it meant. Actually, she was an effective teacher and the Aleuts appreciated her labors, but she did appear to resemble a sea lion more than any other local animal. Her husband, who was good-hearted but smaller than she, was named for a spawned-out salmon. An Aleut male of considerable charm and fine reputation was also named "Hair Seal," probably because he appeared to have short arms. Whenever he was present during the recitation of a story that mentioned hair seals, there was considerable laughter. When visiting in a village, I have often been asked about a man or woman in another village where I have been, who was referred to by the animal name, "Raven," or "Hair Seal" but not the Christian name. This may be the disappearing remnant of earlier days when a name possessed a soul and was truly owned by the person. Invariably polite, the Aleuts might change the name of a local animal or part if a person had the same name and its use could be considered derogatory.

ANATOMICAL TERMS

One area of Aleut culture that had been almost completely overlooked was that of human anatomy. Consequently, a unique and substantial intellectual achievement was not appreciated. The cue to the importance of this area came from an early observation that the Aleuts had a lot of words for anatomy. It speaks highly of the candor and intellectual honesty of the Russian Orthodox priest, Ivan Veniaminov, that he noted this anatomical elaboration in his collection of words:

> The Aleutians have a very extensive anatomical vocabulary. Reference is not made to words like liver, heart, intestines and the like but to several terms, the use of which presupposes familiarity with the details of the structure of the body. *Tugix* large blood vessel, aorta; *cugudagiluq, cunumgudax* places at the back of the neck, the sites of acupuncture. Entire ignorance of anatomical terms makes it impossible for me to translate all of them. Probably such words were formulated from knowledge which, before the arrival of the Russians, the Aleuts had acquired from the study of the interior of a man, either one killed in battle or a dead slave, for the purpose of learning methods of medical treatment.

With this excellent cue for the beginning point, it was possible to investigate the area of anatomical knowledge in the summers of 1948, 1949, 1950, and 1952; and to add more since then (Marsh and Laughlin, 1956). It became clear that the Aleuts still possessed an impressive knowledge of human anatomy and that they surely had an even more highly sophisticated knowledge in earlier days. Their sources of knowledge were the daily butchering of sea mammals, the dissection of sea otters (a true comparative anatomy), autopsy of dead persons in order to find out why they died and for familiarization, and an interest and expertise in health, hygiene, and medical practices including acupuncture and routine blood letting from veins, surgery and suturing, dietary practices, medicaments, and massage. Still another source of information should be inventoried. Aleut empiricism cultivated ability at detailed observation and an experimental turn of mind. Therefore, they made more minute observations about the anatomy of animals killed and also used animal tissues that in many other parts of the world were ignored, such as the gut, gullet, stomach, and the skin of whales' tongues as well as the pericardia of sea lions and brown bears. Aleuts discovered the basic structural similarities between humans and other mammals and used this knowledge for practical purposes to protect themselves and to control their environment.

One outgrowth of Aleut contact with these sources of information is a very large vocabulary of anatomical terms. Furthermore, all these terms are in Aleut. In contrast, an English textbook of anatomy would be considerably diminished if all the Greek and Latin words were removed. Some of the Aleut terms may seem bulky or merely descriptive, but such is still the case with some of our English terms, such as the sterno-cleido-mastoid muscle, no part of which is either technical or rendered in English.

Many anatomical terms are, in themselves, anatomical, such as the eyes of the sacrum (the bone between the two hip bones at the base of the spinal column). This was also a fixed site for acupuncture. The point to be pierced was first marked and a pinch of skin was raised, into which the perforation was made. In another form of acupuncture, two dots are marked on the skin over the internal organ to be treated. A pinch of skin is then raised and the lancet is run through the pinch of skin, entering at the point of one dot and protruding through the other. One objective was to let out "air." Blood letting is closely related to acupuncture and was still practiced in the 1950s. It was performed chiefly on men, and on those between the ages of 20 and 40. Only male doctors can let blood, which probably explains why this is seldom done on women, since women's blood would be unclean to a man. Blood is let either at the ankles from the long saphenous vein on the inner surface, or at the inner bend of the elbow. It is performed no more than once a year and always in the same month in which the course of treatment originated, preferably on a windless day. The four sites are used in succession, one a year.

TABLE 9.1   COMPARISON OF ENGLISH AND ALEUT NAMES
FOR ANATOMICAL FEATURES

English	Aleut
Linea alba (tendinous intersection running vertically down middle of abdomen, Latin for "white line")	Milky way (also for the galaxy)
Brachio-radialis muscle of forearm	Daylight of the hand
Eyelashes	Fringes of the eye (*fringe* also means "baleen fibers," as in a baleen whale)
Septum of the nose	Little man of the nose
Tragus (part of cartilaginous part of external ear)	Little man of the ear
Odontoid process of the second cervical vertebra	Little man of the atlas (in English a Greek stem is used to indicate that it is toothlike)
Root of molar tooth	Leg of the tooth
First molar tooth	Tooth third from the wisdom tooth
Third molar/wisdom tooth	Little one farthest in the interior of the house
Whiskers	Same word as for pubic hair
Windpipe/trachea (English *trachea* comes from Greek word meaning "windpipe")	Place of sound/voice
Pericardium	Sac of the heart
Vertebra	Vertebra (also bamboo, a common driftwood)
Bronchial tubes	Little windpipes of the lungs
Pyloric end of stomach	Umbilicus of the stomach
First posterior sacral foramina	Both eyes of the sacrum (dual ending is used to indicate both of them, singular for one)
Caul	*Chigadagh* (rainproof parka) of the baby

The detail to which the Aleuts have carried their anatomical classification may be demonstrated by their nomenclature for musculature and for hair. Muscles are grouped under three forms. The word *kayugh* means "strength of muscle," and describes a muscle as a motor organ and a source of strength. It is applied primarily to the *biceps brachii* of the arm and to the *quadriceps femoris* of the leg. Both of the muscles are large, powerful, and display high relief with large muscle bellies in man. The term *sayutigh* refers mainly to a flat muscle. The term *igachigh* is applied to a long stringy muscle and is also the name for "tendon/sinew."

All terms for hair are in the plural. Head hair is distinguished from pubic hair and beard hair. The same stem is used for pubic and beard hair, a classification that recognizes the common hormonal regulation involved in the form, color, and time of appearance. Heavier body hairs, such as axillary (of which most Aleuts have none or little) and eyebrows, are *cngan* (the singular of this word means "fur"), and fine fuzzy hairs are *cngaquudan*, "tiny little body hairs." The similarity in words is based on similarity in physical appearance. The name of the sea otter is based on this stem, as well as the name for the yarrow plant, used for a medicinal tea, which is furry in its appearance. Ear and nose hairs bear the name *imliliighun*, "those resembling head-hair." Various locks of the head have their designations, "bangs, forelock," "temple-locks," and "sideburns."

As a bone-working people, they distinguish "bone in general," "soft, cancellous, or interior bone," "hard bone or ivory," and "marrow" (as distinct from brains and from spinal cord, a distinction not made in many languages).

Since the Aleut language possesses both singular, dual, and plural endings, its speakers are readily able with simple endings to designate single, paired, and multiple structures. This linguistic feature has probably led them to make certain anatomical observations that are ignored by other peoples. The mandible is referred to in the dual, and one half in the singular. In most animal mandibles that remain unfused at the symphysis (the middle of the chin region), the use of the dual is obvious. However, the Aleuts also extend the dual concept to the human mandible, which is fused into a single bone. The Aleuts were not simply aware of, but were familiar with many aspects of growth and development, such as the fusion of the two halves of the human mandible during late fetal life. They knew that the anterior fontanelle closes over the soft part of the infant's forehead, that the soft bone in the tips of babies' fingers hardens, and that the epiphyses are still detachable from the bones of young animals.

Acupuncture, blood letting, massage, and suturing are all applications of anatomical knowledge. The knowledge employed in childbirth can only be described as sophisticated and effective. Delivery in the squatting position enabled the woman to contribute more to the delivery. The presence of an experienced woman doctor who could manage a breech delivery and secure the afterbirth if it did not detach and come out of the womb naturally helped reduce infant mortality.

ALEUT ALPHABET

The Aleut alphabet, as devised by I. Veniaminov, who worked closely with Ivan Pankov, chief of Tigalda, as well as with other Aleuts, has served an irreplace-

Ра	ре	ри	рi	ро	ру	ры	ря		рѣ	рю	ря
Са	се	си	сi	со	су	сы	ся		сѣ	сю	ся
Та	те	ти	тi	то	ту	ты	тя		тѣ	тю	тя
Фа	фе	фи	фi	фо	фу	фы	фя		фѣ	фю	фя
Ха	хе	хи	хi	хо	ху				хѣ		
Ца	це	ци	цi	цо	цу	цы	ця		цѣ	цы	цы
Ча	че	чи	чi	чо	чу	чу			чѣ	чу	
Ша	ше	ши	шi	шо	шу	шу			шѣ		
Ща	ще	щи	щi	що	щу	щу			щѣ	щю	щѣ
Ѳа	ѳе		ѳi	ѳо	ѳу				ѳѣ		

Аг҃г҃кх	Богъ	God
Канӫнза	Троица	Trinity
Аг҃гнтакх	Спаситель	Savior
Аг҃г҃кагъꙋнакх	Богородица	Virgin
Аꙟгалангадѧнгадᷰадакх	Святый	Saint
Аг҃г҃лмх ангали	Царствiе Небесное	Heavenly Father
Аг҃г҃лмх ёлл	Рай	Paradise
Кꙋгалх ёлл	Адъ	Hell
Танамаг҃г҃	Царь	Czar
Аг҃налмꙋнтакх	Язычникъ	Heathen
Ангнкх	Духъ	Spirit
Анганкх	Душа	Soul
Тѳнѳꙋтачунгакх	Благовѣстiе	Annunciation
Калга-тѳкнх	Священникъ	Priest
Аг҃аснчунгакх	Благодать	Paradise
Аꙟкатаснѧнгакх	Знаменiе	Signs

ALEUT	RUSSIAN
АꙞГА́ЛꙖХ	МОЛИТВЫ
ТАМАДА́ГҀ	Prayers повседневныя:

КАМГАДА́ГННХ ликанх.

Аꙟачꙋбгакх ⱥ) адаминх [нгаиꙋкх] тꙋбманх ҡ) Ампчꙋбгакх ⱥ) Аг҃ꙋбкх! Ампчꙋбгакх ⱥ) адаминх [нгаиꙋкх].

Слава Тебѣ, Боже нашъ, слава Тебѣ!

Ннимаг҃г҃ꙋ! КАГА_талх ꙗгннада нгннх аꙋтакх! Лнгнмх ага_нгꙋдаванлнх о Амянх абанх ꙋнꙋганх акх, ꙋ_снюх чꙋатакх, нгама_насдадкх Нагмннх гю_ꙋтакх, канꙋх анга_гнкх аꙋтакх! ꙗгалнкх нагнгннх г) Тꙋннх а_гадⱥ канꙋх кнкагналмх ꙋꙋнганз нлднз тꙋбманх

Царю Небесный! Утѣшителю, Душе истины, Иже везде сый и вся исполняяй, сокровище благихъ и жизни Подателю, прiиди и вселися въ ны, и очисти ны отъ всякiя скверны, и спаси, Блаже, души наша.

а) ...саꙟанаꙋх ҡ) Тнмасꙗ г) нагмасꙗ.

Fig. 45. A page showing Aleut and Russian words relevant to religious instruction (with English added). The following page illustrates the instructional use of a half page of Aleut with a half page of Russian.

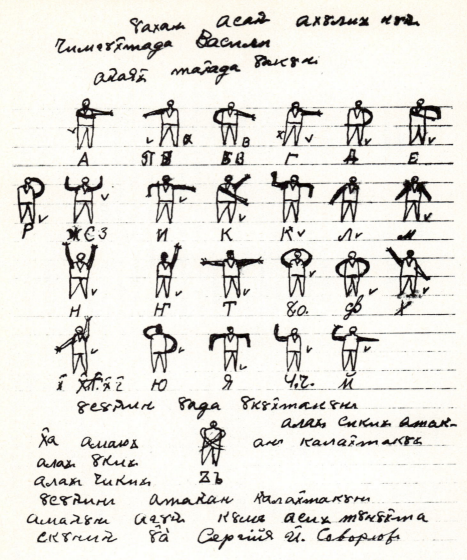

Fig. 46. Aleut semaphore signals are based on the Cyrillic alphabet. These were drawn by one of the inventors, whose name appears at the end of the last line, Sergius I. Sovoroff.

able function in promoting literacy and in facilitating communication between Aleuts and non-Aleuts as well as among Aleuts. The alphabet has established a permanent historical record of Aleut culture and achievement. The preparation of books with half a page in Aleut and the other half in Russian is an efficient method for teaching the reading and writing of one language and introducing a second language at the same time. Veniaminov introduced this system from Siberia where it had been used with success. The enthusiasm with which Aleuts took to writing letters, diaries, and books in both the Atka dialect and in the Fox Islands dialect (with Atka footnotes in some Fox Aleut texts) is testimony to the cultural acumen of the Aleuts. Contemporary Aleut language programs no longer use the Aleut alphabet, largely because it requires a special typeface and no longer has any special advantage compared with our Roman letters.

Aleut may well be the only native American language for which a basic primer included numbers as high as 100,000. The czar is no longer considered to be the God of Land in the Aleutians nor in the Soviet Union, but when the concept was in use, the Aleut language supplied a specific word (Fig. 45) for him. On the other hand, the same word was also used for "spirit" as for "soul." The history of these words and concepts in English is evidence for considerable insight in the Aleut use of a single term.

An interesting Aleut linguistic invention was a semaphore system. This was devised prior to World War I when one of the four men principally responsible for it was working in Unalaska. The headquarters of the Bering Sea Patrol of the U.S. Coast Guard were located there and their ships frequently used a naval semaphore. Using their own alphabet as the base, the Aleuts employed arm positions to indicate each letter of the alphabet they thought necessary, 25 in all. They carefully distinguished *k* from *q*, *n* from *ng*, included bilabials from Russian, and used in one case an arm position to indicate three closely related letters and sounds. Two of these came from Russian and one from Aleut. The figures shown here were drawn by Mr. Sergius I. Sovoroff of Nikolski, one of the inventors (Fig. 46).

One factor in this Aleut invention was the need they had for communication between hunters. Sometimes men engaged in fox trapping were on separate islands or on different sides of the same bay, distances too far for their voices to carry in the wind. Another use was that of informing the people who waited in the village for word of where the mail and supply ship would land. Depending on weather and tide, the ship might come inside Mueller Cove in front of Nikolski Village or much farther away and around a point near the outer opening of Nikolski Bay.

10 / Cossacks

The history of the Russian discovery of Alaska in 1741, and of the exploration and occupation of the Aleutian Islands, is well known in its major outlines and economic aspects. Our purchase of Alaska in 1867 brought with it a rich chapter in human history about citizens whose ancestors were the original discoverers of Alaska many thousands of years earlier. The Aleut word for a Russian is *Cossack*. This is a word that was introduced with early contact, and apparently was based on a minority of Russians who used the title of "Cossack." Both the Aleuts and the Cossacks played important roles in international history, sometimes as pawns and other times as knights. For the earliest Russian hunters, trappers, and traders, the sea cows of the Commander Islands provided an indispensable food supply, and the sea otters of the Aleutians provided the financial reward.

The Russian expansion moved from west to east in the same way that American expansion moved from east to west. The treatment of the native populations was generally similar. Kindliness and killing went hand in hand, and often the hands belonged to the same persons. The first American to meet the Russians in the Aleut village of Unalaska (or Iloolik, if the name based on the curved beach is used), was John Ledyard of Connecticut, who accompanied Captain Cook in 1778. Most of the historical reports follow after this time, and most of them deal more with "headquarters" history than with the "grassroots" history of the Aleuts and Russians. The grassroots history of the Russian and Aleut interaction comes from the Aleut accounts that are astonishingly accurate, from the archeological evidence of Russian skeletons and their associated belongings, from the Aleut language, and from published historical sources.

Accounts of the early Russians are known throughout the Aleutian villages. In 1938, an Aleut told me of the death of several Russians who had chopped down a tall pole that formerly stood by the village. Whiskers Creeklet, a small tributary of Umnak Creek, is named for a bearded Cossack who was drinking from the stream when he fell forward into it and drowned. These Cossacks had walked from a place near High Hill, about 2 kilometers north, where their ship had parted its cable and was stranded on the rocks. Today a small monument house in front of and outside of the churchyard marks and protects the stump of the desecrated pole. It is possible that the man who drowned in the little creek as well as the others, might have been killed by the Chaluka Aleuts.

The Cossacks had killed a number of men on the southern end of Umnak Island

and the Aleuts resented these killings. One man had been shot while holding a sea lion skin shield in front of himself, unaware that a musket ball would pierce the shield. Another man, with no fear, had dressed himself in his finest ceremonial clothes and defied a Cossack party. Thinking they would subdue but not kill him, the Cossacks hit him over the head with a musket. Unfortunately, they hit him too hard, for they killed him and bent the gun barrel as well. An Aleut retelling this event observed that it was the end of the war because the Cossack party had only one gun. This event must have taken place between 1759 and 1763.

In 1948, Marsh and I recorded a story of the successful massacre of an entire Russian party on Chaluka. In various discussions and retellings over the years a few new items came to light, but the integrity of the Aleut account was evident. We were convinced that the early Russians had built a house, variously termed a *yurt* or a *barabara*, and a steam bath on the western end of Chaluka. An excavation in 1952 recovered only one genuinely non-Aleut item, a lead peg in a thin whale-bone piece for a dish. Such vessels were usually stitched with baleen or pegged with bone or ivory. A few items of Russian origin were given to us from time to time by Aleuts who found them on the surface or in their excavations for garbage pits, glass beads, a samovar, and a small iron axe. Such items could have been brought in after the massacre and, therefore, simply provided evidence of contact with Russians. The Aleut story of the massacre remained interesting and credible, but unverified.

THE ALEUT ACCOUNT OF THE MEDVEDEV MASSACRE: "JACOB, SIT DOWN"

The people of Chaluka and other villages of south Umnak were being oppressed by a party of Cossack fur hunters under the leadership of a large, powerful man named Jacob. The men lived in a *barabara* at the western end of the village, and their ship was anchored close by, inside the barrier reef of Nikolski Bay. Only a watch was maintained on the ship; the other men lived on shore. The Aleut men were required to hunt sea otters and to pay tribute. Other parties of *promyshleniks* were fox trapping from stations near other villages on Umnak Island. Finally, a number of men from different villages conspired to massacre the Cossacks. Runners were sent to many villages and two men were selected as the principal agents, Sanhoghtaqagh ("Old Stomach") and Sasiiman ("One Who Kills Many Ducks"). Sasiiman was especially noted for his acrobatic skill, his ability to always land on his feet. Both were strong men.

These two men selected a very fine sea otter pelt, which they rolled up and bound tightly with a sinew cord with a very small knot. They posted three Aleuts outside the door of the Russian house. Jacob was walking back and forth inside the house where his "soldiers" were also gathered. The Aleuts went inside and said to Jacob, in Russian, "Jacob, sit down," and then handed him their gift of the sea otter pelt. He sat down, reached over his head to draw his sword from a ceiling beam, and cut the sinew binding. Pleased with the gift, he stroked the pelt spread on his lap and lay his sword on a table. Sasiiman said "Ta," grabbed the sword and cut his throat while Sanhoghtaqagh held his legs. Jacob pounded the floor with his feet, but Sanhoghtaqagh did not let go. Jacob pushed his way out of the *barabara,* staggered down to the beach, his front red with blood, and died on the beach. The Cossacks inside the house reached to the walls for their weapons. The Aleuts drew their knives from their sleeves, hamstrung them at the knees from behind, and then cut their throats. One man, the cook, remained on board the ship.

The next day, the Aleuts went out to the ship. The cook got down in the hold and held the Aleuts at bay with a spear that he passed back and forth. Finally, the Aleuts picked up Sasiiman and threw him down into the hold when the spear was pointed away. He landed on his feet and quickly cut the cook's throat. However, Sasiiman was cut in the face by the spear. Following this, the ship was dragged to shore and burned. It took a long time to cut the anchor cable. The Aleuts carried ashore all the things of interest to them. Among these were flour, red flannel, and lead. They closed their eyes while carrying the flour, because it got in their eyes and they did not know if it would harm them. They buried the red cloth because of the hazardous meaning of its color. They made knives from the lead and quickly found that it was unsuitable, because it would not hold an edge. The Aleut account of this incident ends with the things they carried ashore and the burning of the ship.

Various details were added with the discussion. The Cossacks had a smithy on the beach, where they worked on the iron used in their lances and other equipment. One Aleut used the Russian word for "saber," while another Aleut used the word *spalga* for the sword of Jacob. It is always observed that the binding on the sea otter pelt was made tight with a small knot so that Jacob could not untie it but would have to use his sword. The names of the leaders, the sequence of events, the hamstringing and the throat cutting, the death of Jacob outside the house, the death of the cook in the ship's hold—these are invariable. Whether Jacob was able to get to a rowboat and begin rowing out to the ship, as indicated in one version, cannot be proven. The place where he died on the beach was shown to us. Obviously, he was trying to get into the rowboat in order to escape to the ship. Clearly, no one escaped.

THE SKELETAL EVIDENCE

The summer of 1970 provided skeletal verification of this bloody struggle. The distal end of a *tibia* (shin bone) projected from a low point on the side of Chaluka, close to the cove. The bone fragment led us to remove what we supposed would be another old Aleut burial. However, the leg bone was connected to a thigh bone that was connected to a hip bone which, in turn, was connected to 13 Russian skeletons (Fig. 47). The bodies had apparently been thrown in upon each other in near random fashion. Heads, arms, legs, and trunk portions were interlaced so that it was difficult to determine which bones belonged to which particular skeletons. Coat buttons had fallen down from the higher to lower bodies. They had obviously been hastily buried in a common grave.

The skeletons themselves reveal a group composed of extremely robust men, attested by the large muscle markings on heavy bones. The bone mineral content of the skeletons, determined by photon scanning, was very high. They had very

Fig. 47. Skeletons of the massacred Denis Medvedev party of 1764 A.D. *A. B. Harper is assembling the vertebral column of one man on a string to preserve the natural sequence.*

prominent noses, a marked contrast with the Aleuts. Three of the men were especially tall and massive. The oldest man was 48 years of age and the youngest was about 21. One of the men was Denis Medvedev. Which one was Medvedev will be known when and if we can secure a list of the ages of the members of this party. Most interestingly, a detailed mapping of the knife cuts by A. B. Harper shows attention to the joints. The neck is the crucial joint in this kind of homicide. This mapping confirmed the manner of their death as described by the Aleuts.

None of the skeletons showed signs of scurvy, and their sound teeth were set tightly in their sockets. This is an important indicator that the Russian party was taken by surprise and that they had not been deprived of food as in a long siege. Other trapping parties that had been under siege for several weeks and were unable to secure fresh foods reported severe cases of scurvy. Most of the teeth were coated with tartar, directly attributable to the tobacco carried in copper snuff boxes. The dental traits and cranial characteristics of one of the men suggest that he may have been a Kamchadal or other Siberian native. His presence is in keeping with the employment of Kamchadals and Koryaks by early Russian fur hunting parties.

An interesting racial difference was the absence of arthritis. Aleut skeletons of the same age usually show some arthritis, and often extensive arthritis. One Russian had a serious bone disease of his lower right leg (*osteomyelitis*), which undoubtedly had troubled him in walking about. It was caused by an infection which in turn might have been caused months earlier by a projectile point.

One Aleut skeleton was found to one side of the Russian skeletons. He had a knife or sword cut on the top of his skull, and may have been an Aleut hostage or interpreter killed in the massacre. His skeleton is of considerable scientific interest because he was an adult of well developed proportions, yet he had two vertebral column defects—*spina bifida* and separate neural arches (see Chapter 2). The head form indicates that he was a late or transitional Paleo-Aleut of the population type appearing just before and overlapping the recent Neo-Aleuts.

The cultural evidence associated with the bodies includes well-made copper boxes, coat buttons with a fancy floral design (Fig. 48), small musket or pistol

Fig. 48. Chaluka, 1970. Coat button (25.5 mm. in diameter) with floral design worn by a member of the Denis Medvedev party of 1764 A.D. who were massacred and interred in Chaluka. An electron-scanning microscope reveals traces of gold plating.

balls, a finger ring, and some fabric of very fine quality with exceptionally long fibers that had been preserved by the copper salts. One man had been buried with two copper boxes, one in each hand. A. P. Okladnikov identified the copper boxes as snuff boxes. He then opened one and found tobacco. The finger ring proved to be a signet ring, much worn, with a Romanoff double-headed eagle design. It was probably used for stamping official letters and other documents. Remnants of five gold points in the crown, detectable by means of an electron scanning microscope, indicated that the gold had a high sulphur content and had probably been manufactured in European Russia. The absence of boot nails, knives, guns, and many more buttons suggests that much of the clothing had been removed along with other possessions.

It appears that a shallow pit had been dug into the midden, the bodies hastily thrown in, and then some midden material (earth, ashes, sea urchin shells, and so forth) thrown over them. In later years some disarrangement had been produced on one side of the pit by a modern Aleut garbage pit and other dislocation done to the site by a curio hunter. The actual remains of this Russian party abundantly confirm the Aleut account, verifying the undeniable accuracy of the rigorously maintained Aleut oral tradition.

THE HISTORICAL ACCOUNT OF THE MEDVEDEV MASSACRE

Widespread interest in Russian discoveries in Alaska led to translation and publication of many early documents. The earliest English publication of Russian discoveries fortunately includes two accounts that bear directly on the fate of Denis Medvedev. These are contained in *Account of the Russian Discoveries Between Asia and America* by William Coxe, 1780, published only 16 years after the massacre.

Denis Medvedev is identified as the Skipper-Apprentice in command of Protassov's vessel. The crew of Protassov's vessel had sent letters to Unalaska on December 8, 1763. Glotov, on his return from Kodiak Island, had landed on Umnak and had discovered the bodies on July 5, 1764.

He discovered the remains of a burnt vessel, some prayer-books, images, &c.; all the iron work and cordage were carried off. Near the spot he found likewise a bathing room filled with murdered Russians in their clothes. From some marks, he concluded that this was the vessel fitted out by Protassoff; nor was he mistaken in his conjectures (Coxe, 1780, p. 119).

Alarmed at the fate of his countrymen, Glotov returned to his ship, held a consultation, and then had a series of adventures in which he was fired on by Aleuts using firearms. Since Glotov did not bury the Medvedev party, the next question is, of course, who did? The answer to this and, with it, the identification of the party is given in an historical account of the voyage of Ivan Korovin and the vessel *Trinity* (Coxe, 1780, p. 99). Korovin had lost his vessel at Umnak. He made his way there from Unalaska under attack. On July 21, 1764, Korovin, who had been under attack for several months, put to sea in a 24-foot (7.3-meter) *baidar*:

... which they had constructed in order to make to Protassoff's vessel with whose fate they were as yet unacquainted. Their number was now reduced to twelve persons, among whom were six Kamtchadals.

After having rowed ten days they landed upon the beach of the same island Umnak; there they observed the remains of a vessel which had been burnt, and saw some clothes, sails, and ropes, torn to pieces. At a small distance was an empty Russian dwelling, and near it a bath-room, in which they found, to their inexpressible terror, twenty dead bodies in their clothes. Each of them had a thong of leather, or his own girdle, fastened about the neck, with which he had been dragged along. Korovin and his companions recollected them to have been some of those who had sailed in Protassoff's vessel; and could distinguish among the rest the commander Medvedeff. They discovered no further traces of the remaining crew; and as none ever appeared, we have no account of the circumstance with which this catastrophe was attended.

After having buried his dead countrymen, Korovin and his companions began to build an hut: they were prevented however from finishing it, by the unexpected arrival of Stephen Glottoff, who came to them with a small party by land (Coxe, 1780, p. 99).

From the date of the last letters sent from Medvedev to Korovin and the initial discovery of the bodies, it is clear that the massacre took place between December 8, 1763, and July 5, 1764. The fact that Medvedev could still be recognized by Korovin on July 31 suggests that the massacre took place in the spring of 1764. The bath room referred to was, of course, a steam bath (*banya*), a culture trait still in use at Nikolski as well as other areas of southern Alaska occupied by the Russians. It is interesting that the early Russians maintained this practice wherever they went.

The full picture of the massacre of Medvedev required the articulation of three bodies of evidence, the Aleut account, the skeletons with their associated items, and the historical accounts. The Aleut account is demonstrably accurate.

THE EARLY RUSSIAN PERIOD: 1741–1768

The sequence of discovery and exploitation of the Aleutian Islands by small groups of Russian hunters moved fairly rapidly from west to east. It is a quirk of history that two uninhabited islands should have a strong influence on the well-populated Aleutian Islands. The Commander Islands (Bering and Medni) first played a role as the major provisioning station for the hunting parties, and later, after 1826, they again played a role in Aleut history as permanent homes for Attu and Atka Aleuts who were relocated mostly from the western and central Aleutians.

The sufferings and privations of the early discoverers were astonishing in their magnitude. Twelve men had already died and 20 more were dying when Bering's ship, the *St. Peter*, drifted onto the southeastern coast of Bering Island on its return voyage from Alaska to Petropavlosk. Only the naturalist G. Steller and a few men whom he had persuaded to eat the antiscorbutic plants he collected were able to stand on deck. An anchor was dropped in front of a long, sandy beach. Shortly afterward, when it appeared that everyone could get some needed rest, a strong wind came up and cast the ship on the offshore reef that was being exposed by the outgoing tide and that was now well marked with breakers. Again, the members of the ship gave themselves up for lost since they were too weak to remedy the situation and the vessel would surely break up in a short time under the pounding of the surf. Providentially, a huge wave lifted the ship off the jagged reef and plopped it over into the low-tide "lagoon." In 1938, we relived the same fear that the *St. Peter's* crew had undoubtedly felt. Leaving the site of Bering's grave and the pits of their winter camp, we embarked in a heavily loaded open boat and momentarily scraped on the same reef on our return to the U.S.C.G.S. *Shoshone*. The commander who was at the rudder immediately appreciated the historical revisitation and called out, "That makes two of us."

The sodden and sorrowful details of disease and death that marked the eight months of fight for survival on the island are well recorded in Stejneger (1936), Golder (1925), and Waxell (1952). The pertinence of these records to Aleut history lies essentially in the illustration of the extraordinary difficulties faced by the early Russian explorers and the nature of the accessible food supply on these two launching islands. The Russians neither anticipated nor corrected their diet to prevent scurvy. In fact, they often ridiculed their botanist who nursed many of them back to health with his plants. They were poorly equipped to investigate the Aleutian Islands, especially in such items as waterproof clothing, small boats, and the use of local foods. In these aspects, the Russians were markedly inferior to the Aleuts who considered the Aleutians the world's best place to live, and who would have enjoyed a sojourn on Bering Island amidst one of the world's greatest supplies of sea mammals, fish, and birds.

The existence of the Steller sea cow, *Hydrodamalis gigas*, provided evidence that no one had inhabited the island for a very long time, if ever. The sea cows were large, simple to catch, tasted very good, and their meat preserved well even in hot weather, and even when covered with worms. They ranged in length up to 33 feet (10 meters) and attained a weight of 22,046 pounds (10,000 kilograms). Instead of teeth, they had horny plates for chewing seaweeds, and commonly browsed in the seaweed beds about the shores. The animals were so docile that Steller was able to stroke them on the back as they luxuriated about the shallow, sandy mouths of brooks. Thus they were easily caught with grappling hooks and lines. Fox, sea lions, harbor seals, sea otters and, in breeding season, fur seals also provided sustenance.

The value of the sea otter pelt was already known and consequently many more were killed by Russian parties than were eaten. The survivors took some 900 pelts back to Petropavlosk in 1742. The display of these pelts triggered the Aleutian stampede of fur hunters. Fortunes were made on Bering and Medni Islands, but the sea otter dwindled quickly, and Tolstykh's second expedition (1756–1757) found no sea otters. The sea cow was exterminated in 1768, and a rare, near-flightless bird, the spectacled cormorant, became extinct in the eighteenth century. This model of overexploitation was reenacted in the Aleutian Islands over a longer period of time, with the Aleuts added to the list of endangered species.

Fur companies of modest size and finance outfitted small boats (*shitik*) made of hewn planks that were literally sewn together with willow ties or with hide thongs and wooden pegs. It was customary for such a boat to travel first to Bering Island, where the crew lay in a supply of sea cow meat, before proceeding on to the Aleutian Islands. In the Aleutians—beginning with the Near Islands (Attu,

Agattu, Alaid, Nizki, and Shemya) in 1745—the Russians encountered people
with whom they could not speak and who were not interested in fox trapping.
Aleuts made only minor use of fox and had directed much of their efforts to the
hunting of sea mammals, fish, and birds with the aid of a considerable advantage
in boats. The Russians wanted sea otter pelts, but did not have a good technology
for sea otter hunting. In overall perspective, it appears that the Russians faced the
task of convincing the Aleuts to hunt sea otters for them. The sea otters were not
nearly as important to the Aleuts as sea lions, seals, and fur seals. Hostilities frequently erupted and the Aleuts were usually the losers.

The first encounter in September 1745 on Agattu Island between the Russian
navigator Nevodchikov, Skipper Chuprov, and their party of 45 Russian and
Kamchadal hunters on the one hand, and the Aleuts on the other, led to bloodshed.
Subsequently, many Aleuts were killed and a boy was captured for training as an
interpreter. Belyaev used an iron spike to kill Aleuts and poisoned the porridge
with corrosive sublimate (bichloride of mercury). After their return, these
hunters were tried in court and Belyaev was punished.

It is difficult to procure population numbers from the early accounts and some
bias was almost certainly introduced by the hunters reporting the number of Aleut
survivors at the time of their departure rather than the full number present at the
time of their arrival. Two figures—3000 and 5000—are given for the number of
Aleuts killed in the Umnak–Unalaska area, including the Islands of the Four
Mountains. Glotov and Soloviev together probably killed over 4000 Aleuts.

It is interesting that Glotov describes his first encounter with Umnak Aleuts in
1759 with careful attention to the details of his wounds. The Cossack S. T. Ponomarev and the group leader S. G. Glotov encountered the Umnak Aleuts in 1759
on the Pacific side of the island some 10 kilometers north of Nikolski. Upon their
arrival, the Aleuts met them with darts and lances with chipped stone points
thrown with throwing boards: ". . . they wounded Ponomarev in the right shoulder,
Glotov in the chest and in the left shoulder, the Kamchadal Ignat'i Uvarovsky in
the right leg, Stefan Uvarovsky they beat to death, but the rest the Lord saved
from that. . . ." Subsequently, the Russians gave presents of needles, awls, and
other items and made restitution for a *baidar* they had broken up with its contents.

> And through this their kindness and welcome after their so friendly intercourse
> with them on the two indicated islands (Umnak and Unalaska) was brought by
> them with all the ship's company into subjection under the all powerful hand
> of her imperial majesty and into payment of the fur-tribute. . . ." (translation
> from Russian by G. H. Marsh, June 1951).

The names of the *toyons* (chiefs) on both islands are given, but the villages
are not specified for Umnak. Three chiefs are specified as living at Ikalga Bay
(modern Chernofski) on the west coast of Unalaska, near the north end of Umnak
Pass facing Umnak.

The actual nature of the relations can best be judged by the great uprising of
1763–1764, in which the Aleuts of the Islands of Four Mountains, Umnak, Unalaska, and probably Akutan, coordinated their efforts to drive out the Cossacks and
helped destroy three out of four vessels, all of the Medvedev party, and some of
the other three parties. Because these initial encounters so often led to bloodshed,
relations between the fur hunters and the Aleuts rapidly degenerated. The success

of the Aleuts, however short-lived, depended upon their ability to organize villages for a common enterprise, upon the fact that the Fox Islands were heavily populated, and upon their courage.

No fewer than 167 Russians were on Umnak and Unalaska at the same time. This is the number of Russians, including Kamchadals and Koryaks, known to have sailed from Kamchatka on these four vessels. The vessels involved were: the *Trinity*, owned by Trapeznikov and commanded by Ivan Korovin; the *Zacharias and Elizabeth*, owned by Kulkov and commanded by Alexei Drushinin; the *St. John*, owned by Jacob Protassov and commanded by Dennis Medvedev; and the *Andrea and Natalia*, owned by Terenty Chebaevskoi and commanded by Stephen Glotov. The *Andrea and Natalia* was the only vessel to return to Kamchatka. The other three were destroyed.

Glotov commanded the only remaining vessel and the survivors of the other ships eventually made contact with him. Glotov began retaliatory strikes of significant dimension. He was aided by the arrival on September 16, 1764, of Ivan Maximovich Soloviev, commander of the *Holy Apostles Peter and Paul*. Glotov and Soloviev killed all the people in some of the villages on the Islands of Four Mountains, Umnak, and Unalaska. The most frequently recounted event is the killing of nine Aleuts with a single shot. At the village of Kashega, Soloviev tied 12 Aleuts, front-to-back in single file, and fired a musket into the first. The bullet lodged in the ninth Aleut. The Aleuts had no weapon, lance, harpoon, or arrow that could penetrate nine persons.

The Aleuts were locked into an untenable position because of their dependence upon the sea, and especially on the coastline. They had no place to go other than between islands. When their food supplies were destroyed or taken, and the able-bodied hunters killed, starvation ensued for the other members of the population. Old people, of whom they were many, and infants could not long sustain the resistance. Unlike the Nez Perce Indians who could retreat into Canada, the Modoc Indians who took refuge in the Lava Beds, or the Tlingit Indians who could retreat into the forests, the Aleuts had no refuge.

By the time of Captain Cook's visit to Unalaska in 1778, most of the Aleuts from Attu to the Alaska Peninsula and the Shumagin Islands were subdued and the original population of 16,000 reduced by one-third or more, possibly by one-half. The Aleuts never recovered.

Early Russian contacts with the Aleuts at the village level were numerous and continuous. The Russians were males, young (between 20 and 50 years of age), strong, and enterprising. They were dispersed in small groups, often 10 or 11, less often 25, and they traveled between villages and along the coastline on foot, in *baidars*, and in ships. The Aleuts learned the Russian language very early, as indicated in their request to Jacob to "sadiis." By 1778, the Russians were dispersed over most of the islands and on the Alaska Peninsula. It is likely that there were more Russians in direct contact with Aleuts between 1759 and 1799 than at any time after the eighteenth century, and it is also likely that there were more Russians in total numbers prior to the nineteenth century. The most effective acculturation took place at the village level between the small parties of Russian hunters and the villagers in the first 30 to 40 years of contact.

Change in the distribution of Russians took place continuously with the general undeniable trend being the assembly of more of the Russians at headquarter stations, such as Unalaska, St. Paul in the Pribilofs, Kodiak, and Sitka (New Archangel), and fewer in the villages. There never were many Russians in Alaska at any one time—never more than 1000 and more often 500–600. Thus, only 20 ships hunting in the Aleutian chain with total complements numbering around 40 persons, meant some 800 Russians in contact with the Aleuts at the village level. At times, there were more than 20 Russian vessels in the chain and along the Aleut portion of the Alaska Peninsula. Often, some were in transit to or from Petropavlosk.

The schools and hospitals came long after the Aleut population was reduced to less than an eighth of its former size. The various charters of the Russian-American Company, beginning with 1799, provided for the maintenance of the villages, limited the number of men (one-half of those between 18 and 50) who were required to serve the company, and limited the length of service to three years, as of 1821. However, the number of villages and the numbers of people had already been severely reduced. Furthermore, the relocation of Aleuts to the Pribilof Islands was very hard on these Aleuts and significantly reduced their length of life.

RUSSIAN TRAITS AND CHANGES

The meeting of Russians and Aleuts was one of contrast and similarity. The Russians were newly arrived, emissaries of a socially and politically complex society that was expanding to the east. As a major European and Asian power, they were in competition with other European powers expanding to the west. The Aleuts were an intact society that had been in the Aleutian Islands for several thousand years and had perfected a marine culture that was remarkably adapted to its rich environmental resources. It had elaborated genuinely intellectual interests. They held a near-monopoly on sea otter hunting from kayaks which the Russians were quick to appreciate. However, the sea lion, harbor seal, fur seal, and whales were of considerably more use to the Aleuts and were necessary to the construction of their boats and clothing, and for food as well. Aleut boats were complex in structure and required sea lion skins. This was true for both the large open *baidar* and the small closed *baidarka*. They were easily damaged and required a long time to manufacture. The Russians could only barter for sea otter pelts or convince and persuade the Aleuts to hunt for them. Concentration on sea otter hunting was disruptive to the ecological foundations of the Aleut population and seriously depleted the supply of both sea otters and of Aleuts.

Needles and awls, kettles, knives and axes, cloth and beads, tobacco, and tea were offered as gifts to the Aleuts and in barter for skins. The Aleut men immediately appreciated knives and axes, though with the qualification that they used the axes like adzes, a habit that persisted well into the nineteenth century. Swords, muskets, and lances (iron-tipped) did not move between the two groups. Swords did not fit the habits of the Aleuts and, like muskets, the Russians did not trade them. Some muskets fell into the hands of the Aleuts and were used against the Russians on a few occasions, but the Aleuts could not secure enough of them or enough powder to make them a dependable weapon. The Aleuts had their own lances, most of which they could throw with their throwing boards. They used harpoons and lances, bows and arrows, and clubs and knives most commonly.

Copper boxes and beads were attractive but not essential to the Aleut economy. The Russians appear to have been in short supply of many of the items. A repeated complaint of the Aleuts is that only one needle was allowed for a village, or a few at most, and if that needle were broken, the people were held liable. A similar complaint, more specific, is that only one musket was allowed for a village. Thus the village of Natuqagh, south of Chaluka, had one musket that they were to fire as an alarm in the case of an attack by Atka Aleuts. This relates to a later period around 1800 A.D.

The most sublime introduced trait was, of course, the steam bath (*banya*). It is not known when the Aleuts began building their own, but it is certain that Medvedev used a steam bath at Chaluka and it is probable that most of the Russian parties built steam baths. This trait as well as the beater, or switch, used to stimulate the flow of blood, were taken over by the Aleuts. With time, the Aleuts put doors in the sides of their houses and added at one end a *kalador*, or entry chamber. Fireplaces with mud and wood chimneys were installed and the old roof entry with notched log ladder was abandoned.

Significant changes took place in boats. More of the two-hatch *baidarkas* came into use; they were faster, had a greater carrying capacity, and were more suitable for long trips. The Aleuts later innovated a three-hatch *baidarka*. Izmailov, commander of the Russian party at Iloolik in 1778, came to visit Captain Cook in a three-hatch *baidarka*. Like all administrators, he sat in the middle while the Aleuts paddled. Corporal Ledyard, who was sent by Cook to establish contact with the Russian post, was transported in a two-hatch *baidarka*, lying on his back completely inside the vessel, between the two paddlers.

Sleds, cloth sails, and shoe lasts were introduced, although the period cannot yet be determined. The Russians used sleds with broad runners, which the Aleuts made of whalebone. Such sleds were used in the winter time for hauling. At Atka, they were used, with sails, for hauling goods between the village on Korovin Bay across a frozen lake to the Nazan Bay side of the island. Sails and rudders were tried on *baidarkas*, with the rudder control operated by hands rather than by feet.

Among the materials that the early Russians used were the Aleut *baidars*, various foods, and selected items of clothing. Aleut boots were eventually made on wooden lasts and a kind of mass production was instituted under the Russian-American Company. Medical treatment of various sorts was genuinely appreciated by the Russians, and Veniaminov describes this. The Russians supplied bread and the Aleuts then supplied the other ingredients for a wide variety of baked pies, including fish and bird eggs.

The Aleut reinterpretation or revision of Russian traits reveals much of the Aleut culture. Chess was quickly adopted and played. I found that in all cases the queen had to be on the left of the king, who was an "old man," rather than on the right in the usual opening position for the white queen, because a woman should not be on the right side of a man. When glass bottles were introduced, the Aleuts made a baby's nursing bottle by filing a hole in the bottom on one side to admit air, and attaching a nipple to the mouth. The nipple was made

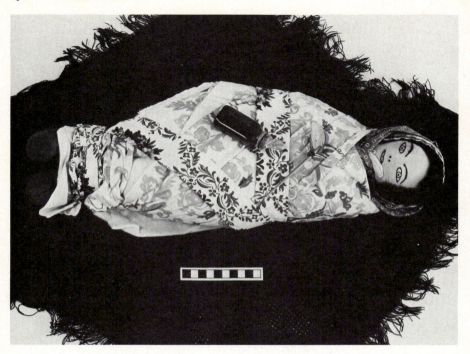

Fig. 49. Large doll dressed in Russian-period style. Patilka *(bottle) with stitched nipple for milk (or flour and water), and feeding spoon of mussel shell with wood handle.*

of two pieces of sealskin sewn together like the finger of a glove (Fig. 49). The crossbow survived as a toy, as in Greenland. The yoke, however, continued in use for carrying two buckets of water or other balanced loads through the 1950s.

It appears that no area of Aleut life and culture was unaltered by Russian influence, at least to a slight degree. We do not know how many of the changes took place in the early period of contact, although we know that the reduction of the population and the concentration on sea otter hunting had profound effects. In the latter part of the eighteenth century, there were many small fur trading companies, sometimes fighting with each other. The number of sea otters, and probably sea lions as well, was declining. By the time the clerics arrived in approximately 1795 and the Russian-American Company was formed in 1799, the Aleut population as a whole was well beyond the point of no return. Records of the priests and of company officials were better than those of early fur hunters, but there were many fewer village activities as well as villagers to record.

11/Modern life in an ancient village

The last 200 years of history have been the most traumatic for the Aleuts, and of these the last 40 years have been the most destructive to Aleut cultural traditions. Are Aleut communities still Aleut or have they lost so much of their old characteristics that they are simply isolated collections of individuals with no place to go? Is it possible that the loss of recognizable traits, kayaks, umiaks, harpoons, and stone oil lamps is not reflected in the internalized behavior patterns of being an Aleut? The existence of Aleutian communities such as Nikolski, Akutan, and Atka represents historical persistence—a tendency toward cohesiveness that expresses itself in the behavior of the people, even though the material traits have changed greatly. Each village is different in many ways, yet there are common elements. Atka is situated on a magnificent bay with many islands and has both Atka and Attu speakers living there. It is the most isolated. Akutan was profoundly affected by the whaling station and its proximity to Unalaska, but maintains a vigorous community. Unalaska has long been a commercial and administrative center, at one time headquarters for the Bering Sea Patrol of the U.S. Coast Guard, a hospital, and also enjoyed the benefits of the Jesse Lee Home. One of its students is now a member of the board of trustees of a university. St. Paul and St. George have, of course, been configured by their role in the fur seal industry. Effective Aleut leadership has come from all the villages in spite of the situational variations. An examination of which traits and behaviors persist, and which ones have been lost or seriously altered suggests a high degree of tenacity and adaptability that is one of the old hallmarks of Aleut culture.

CHALLENGES TO ALEUT CULTURE

The major challenges to Aleut culture read like a chamber of horrors: massacres, introduced diseases, epidemics, tidal waves, foreign invasion and captivity, evacuation from the islands, relocation, the imposition of foreign languages and administrators, food shortages, and the loss of natural resources.

Major environmental hazards continue with visible effects. To these must be added the external reordering of life that is now more closely tied with events in Washington, D.C., and all the agencies that report to Washington, and simultaneously, the agencies of the State of Alaska. Within each community, there are the problems of interpersonal relations that are more nearly internal affairs, but annually they are resolved by external pressures as well as by internal readjustments.

CHARACTERISTICS OF ALEUT SOCIETY

Steam Baths   Characterizing Aleut society and modern life is difficult without citing all the variations and exceptions to each generalization. Some institutionalized activities are sufficiently uniform to provide a partial picture of modern life. The steam bath is an institution in the real sense of the word and one of the great linchpins of Aleut village society. It is one of the key places to study Aleut society and to become scouringly clean at the same time.

On the occasion of his nameday or birthday, or in honor of a returning friend or relative, or because the weather has been soggy or windy for too long a time, a man may "cook" (prepare) a steam bath. This means collecting driftwood for the fire that heats the stones and hot water, hauling the water, and collecting dried grass for the floor of the steaming room and the floor of the dressing room—a task ideally designed for old women. Beginning in the afternoon, a fire is built under a box of large cobble stones that are carefully selected to avoid those that crack and shatter when doused with hot water. In the box, a drum of water is heated. When the fire has cooked the stones for about four hours and most of the smoke has disappeared through a small trap in the low roof, the roofhole is closed and the bath is ready.

The host sits by the door to the inner chamber where he can ladle hot water onto the hot stones to make steam, reach the cold water barrel to replenish the hot water drum, or mix hot and cold water in a basin for a man who is finished and wants to wash before he leaves. The guests arrive, having been invited by a small boy who comes to the house and tells them that the bath is ready. They take off their clothes and enter the steam chamber. One at a time, each man climbs onto a low bed generously padded with sweet-smelling grass and proceeds to call for hot water on the rocks and to beat himself with a little soft-grass broom. He may, if he is a real old-timer, sing an Aleut song as he rhythmically lashes himself. He may also call for more and more water on the stones until the heat has become so intense that all the men sitting on the floor are forced to lie down or to crawl out on hands and knees. A common temperature is about 55°C. at head height while sitting, and temperatures occasionally go around 82°C.

Sore joints and muscles relax as the inner marrow of the bone and the brain are slowly and narcotically cooked. Men discuss all sorts of matters, such as hunting incidents, reports of trips, fishing, jokes, and a variety of recollections. Occasionally, an old Aleut word appears in this relaxed context that would ordinarily not be used in common conversation.

The women look forward to steam baths quite as much as the men, although they come later when it is not so hot. Hair and face are doused with cold water, so as not to be overcome by the heat. Pleasantries and exclamations of satisfaction and appreciation are exchanged along with reciprocal back rubs and hair washes. Should one become too still in complete relaxation, she is quietly nudged to be sure she has not fainted. Steaming and dousing with cold water may also be used to prepare a pregnant woman for delivery. After bathing, drying off, and reclothing, the people go home to drink large amounts of tea.

The steam bath is one of the benefactions of Russian culture, for there does not appear to be any prior archeological evidence, although some sort of dry sweat bath may have been used.

Food Gathering Beach seining for salmon is another social activity that binds the community. Although the seine may be individually owned, everyone who helps haul in the net receives a portion. The owner of the seine is entitled to a few extra salmon. The seine is folded onto the stern of a dory, rowed out in a semi-circle and brought back to shore about 100 feet (30.5 meters) away. The villagers then haul in on both ends and the water becomes a dense mixture of mist and writhing salmon bodies. Once safely on shore, the people break the necks of the salmon and throw them up higher on the shingle beach. Finally, the fish are divided and the people walk home carrying salmon on either hand, slowly and happily. Some are eaten soon, some are dried, or salted, or dried and smoked. Drying salmon requires careful attention because of rain and subsequent rot. People often split the salmon, remove the backbone, but leave the tail intact so it can be hung over a log rack. Some people use a *sulaya*, a little roofed structure that is open on all sides and has the drying racks in front of it. If rain comes, the salmon are hustled in under the roof and brought out again when the weather improves. Drying, like smoking, is an individual or household activity.

The village fish trap in Umnak Creek had been a mainstay of Nikolski life for so many years that it requires mention. It has been alluded to by Turner (1886) and Jochelson (1933) and in all likelihood antedates the arrival of the Russians here, as well as elsewhere. It was abandoned during the 1950s when the salmon runs declined markedly. The upper dam was built of planks lain against a large, horizontal log spanning the stream. Interestingly, a plank was removed at least one day a week so that adequate numbers would ascend into the lake for spawning. The lower dam was built of stones and contained a conical wood entry port, much smaller at the inside opening so that salmon could not find their way back out. These two dams were placed about 20 feet (6.1 meters) apart (see Fig. 50). Each morning, the "divider," a man often accompanied by a young assistant, walked in with a gaff and threw the salmon up on the bank. When I described a faster method of using a net that I had seen on Bering Island, an old Aleut told me that they had formerly walked them out with a net but that this was more fun. A representative of each household came to the bank and stood in a ragged circle about the pile of salmon. The "divider" then picked the salmon up, two at a time, and dropped them in front of the householder, going about the circle until the supply was exhausted. Larger households received an additional share or shares, and one that had sufficient salmon might give its share to another.

Sea lion hunting has long been an activity with a community distribution, although the hunting itself is done by relatively few men. As few as one or two dories might go out to a sea lion rookery and shoot six or eight young sea lions and then boat them for the return home. Upon arriving at the beach, the men butcher them, and the women might work on a special part they desired, such as a stomach for a storage container or the flippers for boot soles. The chunks of meat are then placed on an upturned boat or simply on the rocks and everyone

Fig. 50. Nikolski, 1952. Division of salmon taken from trap. The lower stone wall of trap is at the back of the "divider," the plank upper wall of the trap on his right. Each pile of salmon goes to a household. Each week planks are removed from the trap to permit salmon to continue on up to Umnak Lake for spawning.

may come and take what he wants. The hunters and boatmen could take larger amounts and the hunter could take the hide if he wished. The appearance of villagers who help beach the boats, haul up the sea lion, and help with the butchering is as certain as it is informal.

In contrast to beach seining or to the distribution of sea lion meat, eggs are handled in a quite different manner, although they are as seasonally scheduled as the salmon. Gull eggs and eider eggs are especially good, fried or as an ingredient in egg bread, fried bread, cakes, or pies. A man and his partner, or a family, might go egg collecting. Taking only a few from each nest, they may collect 80 to 300. If a large number is collected, some are given to other families, following a distributional matrix that involves kinship, proximity, and need in a pattern adjusted to the day and hour.

Similarly, on Berry Day, August 19th, many people go collecting moss berries and salmon berries. However, the berries collected belong to the individual or to the family. It provides an example of an event with a common response focused at one time but with little necessary cooperation.

Camping   Camping takes on new forms every few years, but the practice retains a flavor dating back to the terraces on which the villages are situated. A man will build a *barabara* at some abandoned village site which provides good fishing, or sealing, or goosehunting. In the summer, the people tend to disperse to these camps. The advent of the outboard engine has facilitated such trips, and the increase in the use of the Honda has made many of them even more accessible because it is possible to return to the village for a church service or a steam bath, pick up some supplies, and return to the camp. These camps are used in winter as well as summer. They serve a great many functions. Aside from the food resources, they provide recreation, privacy, a place for withdrawal from the higher voltage village life, and a change. They are escape valves that all appreciate, and the children especially look forward to new places to play and new beaches to comb for Japanese glass fish net floats, crab floats, buoys, bottles, pieces of furniture, toys, and the other things that float from passing ships or foreign shores. Teenagers going out with their peers are relieved from babysitting and badgering adults and get an opportunity to practice new skills and independence.

Formal Relationships   The Aleuts, of all the three dialect groups, are amazingly formal in their interpersonal relationships. Under no conditions do they take each other for granted nor presume upon tenuous relationships. Their habits of politeness and of borrowing provide illustration. They greet each other with acceptable animal name (nickname), proper given name, or relationship term. They are agreeable and place great value on not showing anger or other strong emotion. They do not like to say no or reject a request, and the answer to a request requires careful examination to find a negative message. One form of being polite and preserving anonymity is to refer to a source of information or the major figure in an incident as "someone." "Someone said" or "Someone told me" is one of the most recurrent forms in common speech.

The "best friend" relationships, the namesakes, the genealogical pathways, and the adoptive relationships all relate each individual to every other individual in a village. These inherited and designated relationships help hold the community together.

They know that the very next day they may be working together hauling in a net, cutting up a sea lion, or launching a dory. Men who have gotten into a fight —a rare event—may be working together rounding up sheep and they know that they must and will get along with each other. The first encounter with their game of gossip leaves the listener astonished and certain that the village will collapse in a holocaust of cudgeling and blood letting. The village, however, does not even have to pull itself together. It is designed to run this high voltage load through its circuits and carry on.

Village Political Organization   Formal political organization consists of an elected village council with the standard posts of President, Vice President, Secretary, and council members. In Akutan, the posts of First Chief, Second Chief, and Third Chief are still preserved, and they operate with efficiency. The visitor who needs a house speaks to the First Chief. Shortly thereafter, a house is located and the Third Chief is pumping oil into the barrel and making any other preparations needed for occupancy.

The village health aide may take pulse and blood pressure, hand out aspirin, call the Alaska Native Service Hospital in Anchorage for advice, or, as in Akutan, she may deliver the babies with skill and save the varied problems of sending someone to Anchorage. Forty years ago, it was rare for a child to be delivered in a hospital, except in Unalaska.

The village storekeeper, *prekaska*, is a functionary of considerable local knowledge, somewhat like the editor of a small-town newspaper. He must anticipate what people want to buy, how much, and the state of their finances. With two major shipments a year, it is crucial that the essentials be ordered. In this same schedule pattern, there is a real inconvenience when a mail-order house sends the wrong item.

The school teacher and his or her spouse, who are employed as maintenance personnel, spend more time teaching and less time in administration of village affairs than 20 years ago (Laughlin, 1951, Report to Governor Gruening, "Decline of the Aleuts"). The village council now runs independently of the school teacher and the postmaster.

Russian Orthodox Church   The church—Russian Orthodox with Aleut innovations—is invariably a well-kept building. Some of the icons within the church are handsome and a few date back to medieval Russian monasteries. Many are nonmetallic, unframed, and were formerly rolled for transporting in *baidarkas*. The psalmist and his assistant open the church for services, which are conducted with dignity and excellent singing. The Easter service is especially well done, the singers well rehearsed and full voiced. The bells of the Nikolski church of St. Nicholas, the Thaumaturge, are rung during services by one man who cleverly rings all five by use of hands, body, and legs. Officials of the church, and others who pay a fee, may be buried within the churchyard; the membership otherwise is buried in the nearby cemetery, although in two villages the cemetery is a quarter of a mile (403 meters) off. Twenty feet (6.1 meters) in front of the churchyard is a small rectangular house, Monument House (see Fig. 51). This house marks and protects the stump of the tall pole that stood here when the first Russians arrived. It was so tall that a raven on top of it looked like a wren from the ground. The Russians chopped it down to make a house and all of them died as a consequence. Anyone who touches the house in a mood of challenge or disbelief will suffer fearfully.

Cooking   The women maintain superb skills in cooking, especially in breads, pastries, meats, fish, birds, and soups. Whether with wood stove or oil stove, they manage the proper heat for pies, cakes, cookies, or fish, and they alternate old Aleut-Russian recipes with the most recent ones given on the packages. A recipe for eider egg bread requires four fresh eider eggs, well beaten, four heaping tablespoons of flour, poured gradually into a well-greased pan. This recipe dates from the days when there was very little flour available and sugar was rare. Sugar can be added (one tablespoon) if desired. Many reef foods are commonly used—sea urchins, mussels, limpets, chitons, and octopus. Most of these are best if soaked in water overnight and cooked very little. In soups with fish, especially red salmon and silver salmon, they are magnificent. Various kinds of fry bread are more tasty if they are cooked in seal oil. *Aladixs*, shaped like figure eights, are an unleavened bread fried in seal oil. If made with gull eggs, which are larger than eider eggs, they are very rich and solid. They should be dipped in seal oil that is naturally rendered from the blubber, not fried.

Birthday or nameday parties are one of the supreme achievements of Aleut cooking and social life. No matter which village or what time of year, child or adult man, a profusion of excellent food with rich pastries is set forth. Since only 8 or 10 persons can be seated at one time, successive shifts of guests are called by

Fig. 51. Linguist G. H. Marsh standing by the Monument House, outside the churchyard of St. Nicholas, Nikolski, Umnak. This small house protects the stump of the tall pole standing here when the first Russians arrived, and it protects the people from the dangers of touching the pole. Legend has it that Nikolski will survive, and its Aleuts, as long as the pole stump remains.

runner. Each time they sit down, each cake or pie is complete—no partial servings are permitted to appear. The plate of cookies must be restacked and the tea or coffee kept hot. No guest can resist sampling everything, and if he must attend two birthday parties on the same day, he staggers home in pleasant distress.

Family Life   Family life is metered and secure. Children must learn and they acquire early a genuine respect for their elders within the household and for all elders in the village. Since Aleuts build their own homes and lumber is expensive to ship in, their houses tend to be small. It may be necessary for four people to sleep in one small room, and this requires a tactful use of space. Discipline is spoken, spanking is rare. Children are usually dismissed when visitors come, and they soon learn to watch and not interfere. Teenage girls tend to band together and may host a Fourth of July dance. They make the food and refreshments and collect the records or tapes to be used. They may also go camping together.

Most Aleut children are partially bilingual, speaking Aleut with their parents in the home and English in the school. A complicating problem is the widening gap between the older generations and the younger ones. The Aleut language has been changing, partly in response to the imposition of Russian and English, and partly to internal linguistic changes that have to do with reduplication and other processes of language change. One consequence of this is the inability of younger

Aleuts to communicate with their grandparents in Aleut. If they have been away a few years, they may not be able to discuss complex matters with their own parents in Aleut. All parents now want their children to learn good English and to an extent, they may use more English as a way of encouraging the child to use English. There is much less Aleut story-telling in the home than even 20 years ago, and with this lapse go many Aleut forms that require redundancy to learn.

Children were formerly warned against the "outside men" who might get them if they strayed too far or did not return home before dark (Ransom, 1947). Now they are more often concerned with contaminated water, of liver flukes in the lake, or school attendance.

The young unmarried Aleuts face a demographic crunch. There is a shortage of marriageable females of appropriate age and unrelatedness in a small village. One family name includes 27 percent of the people of Nikolski. This kind of disproportionate reproduction is as interesting socially as it is genetically. One social consequence is a partial accentuation of the mate shortage because they, and their children, cannot marry each other. Four young unmarried men have no mates available in their age class, and five men have lost wives and have been unable to marry.

Young girls have been migrating in excess of young men, often after completing high school at Mt. Edgecumbe. Occasionally, an Aleut girl marries a white man; and more rarely, an Aleut man marries a white girl. In two cases, Aleuts have married Indians, a distinctly post-World War II phenomenon.

Modern Communication   Communication between households is now enhanced by the use of walkie-talkies, usually three-volt hand-held models. These are carried in the dories so that the boatmen may advise the people on shore of their safe arrival on an offshore island, of the number of sea lions they are bringing home and so forth. Each morning in Nikolski, a number of men, about five or six from different houses, check in with each other. Their conversational round includes weather, plans for the day, whether or not their stove went out during the night, and it may be given in either English or in Aleut. This is a local development in Nikolski and does not appear in Akutan or in Atka nor in Unalaska. Children do not use walkie-talkies, but the teenagers and women are familiar with them and may receive calls if they happen to be present when the calls come over the wire.

The Honda has become a mainstay of life in Nikolski. As previously indicated, it is useful for hauling loads, beachcombing, visiting the camps, rounding up sheep, and finding the horses for rounding up sheep from distant areas; it also provides entertainment for the teenagers and a goal for younger children. Permission of the mother or father is necessary and also money for gas is usually obtained from the parents. No children or teenagers own boats, although men frequently take a young boy to help with the boat and to provide him with training. The shift to outboard engines from the old Clift inboards has left only one dory, little used, with an inboard. At the other end of the range, the shift from dory to skiff has only begun; whereas, in other villages, skiffs have become more common. The expense of Hondas, dories, and outboard engines is a major capital cost with a return primarily in food items (halibut, eggs, sea lion) and in driftwood for firewood, but not in a commercial return.

INTERVILLAGE COOPERATION

Intervillage organization now exists in the form of the Aleut Corporation and the Aleutian–Pribilof Islands Association. The Chaluka Corporation participates in many ways, as do the other village corporations. The reorganization that began in the 1930s is an important precursor. The Alaska Native Claims Settlement Act of 1971 that established regional and village corporations has facilitated representation in various claims against the government. The Nikolski Aleuts never received adequate restitution for losses suffered in their village during World War II, nor have the Atka and Attu Aleuts. The resources of the Aleut domain have always been the most exposed to foreign as well as domestic depletion, whether in whales, salmon, fur seals, or sea otters. The list of deprivations, of obligated services never rendered adequately, if at all, and of tangible and intangible losses is a long and fascinating list. The United States distinguished itself among nations by making treaties with native peoples and these treaties, many years later, have often provided the basis for redress (Washburn, 1971). However, the Aleuts were placed in an uncertain category because Alaska was purchased from Russia by treaty with the Russian government.

Many court cases have come and gone and more will appear in the future. Some five or six points usually appear in one form or another and these points, recurrent questions, may be used to summarize and focus on the kinds of questions to which the Aleuts have had to respond and about which they have had to assemble and organize evidence.

1. *Ethnic identity: Who are the Aleuts?* This question arose in the 1960s with the proposition that if Aleut and Eskimos were not Indians, they therefore were not entitled to provisions made for Indians. By letter and deposition, it was pointed out that the term *Indian* had been applied to all the original inhabitants of the New World, along with the belief that if you had seen one of them, you had seen them all. There are humorous aspects to this as well. After giving a lecture at the University of New Delhi, I was gently asked by the chairman if there were not a better term for the indigenes of America, for many of the audience felt that *they* were the Indians.

It is usually necessary to characterize the Aleuts and to discuss their distinctions from Eskimos and Indians, such as the kinds of data presented in Chapter 2. Continuity and time depth invariably must be established. The fact that the teeth, skeletons, and many traits on these can be followed back through time establishes the reality of the Aleut people's existence as a people. This group of questions is a pleasure to deal with because the Aleuts can demonstrate a longer continuous existence as an identifiable people in one place than any other people in the world. The admixture that has taken place has not erased the original configuration, but has simply added to the population variation.

2. *Do Aleut village communities have decision-making capability?* This question involves discussing the ways in which Aleut communities actually operate, their informal as well as formal social organization. Leasing land adjacent to a native village can and should be preceded by consultation with the village officers

and council, and whoever they delegate to discuss and review the matter. The fact that various commercial enterprises settled in Aleut villages without permission does not obscure the fact that village communities were interested and competent to render a decision. There has never been a group of Aleuts, including hunting parties as well as village communities, that did not have an identifiable leader, and the qualifications of his authority are basic aspects of the organization of the community.

3. *Use of natural resources*: The question often comes up in the form of questioning either the actual dependence of Aleuts on the plants, animals, birds, fish, and invertebrates, or whether they made a skilled and serious use of such resources. These data are given in Chapter 4, as well as in other places. The vast amounts of animal debris testify to the extensive use of the reefs, of birds (and the many kinds of birds), of sea mammals, and so forth. The single greatest financially calculable loss to the Aleuts has probably been that of the sea otters, greater than the fur seals. The sea otter, after all, is basically why Russia owned Alaska and one of the reasons why we purchased Alaska. The reason that sea otters may be ranked above fur seals is that their membership in the Aleutian ecosystem has many more connections than that of the fur seals. There are complex and sustained relationships with the marine algae, sea urchins, and other members of the complex food chains on a year-round basis. Sea otters are slow colonizers; like the Aleuts, they prefer to remain where they are.

These three summary points include a giant pyramid of subsidiary questions, many of which concern the health, economics, and government services rendered in past years. As previously mentioned, the length of life is one objective, tangible, and significant measure of the actual health and welfare of the Aleuts and other people. The reduction of length of life among the Pribilof Aleuts is one of the most remarkable in the world. The causes and contributions of this phenomenon must be measured in terms of the actual results.

One of the landmark decisions in favor of Aleuts was handed down on June 9, 1978, by the Indian Claims Commission. The plaintiffs, "members of the Aleut Tribe of Indians residing on St. Paul and St. George," were awarded $11,239,604 in recognition of the Government's obligation to provide fair compensation and sufficient goods and services to the Pribilof Aleuts during the 76-year period in question (1870–1946). This is a concrete example of how modern life depends, one way or another, on the past life and lives of Aleuts (Laughlin and Harper, 1976). Parts of this case actually run back to the early 1950s.

At the time of Jochelson's visit in 1909–1910, most of the Nikolski Aleuts lived on top of the Chaluka midden. He therefore excavated at other sites on the south end of Umnak Island. He did find several well-informed Aleuts in Nikolski and recorded a great many stories. At the time of my 1938 visit, the young boys still played with throwing boards and darts. In 1948, only two kayaks remained, a single- and a double-hatch, the crossbow was used as a toy, and no one played with throwing boards. The village had both a chieftainship system and a village council, and there were a number of men and women who were both good linguistic and good ethnological informants.

Babies were still delivered by a skilled midwife and the village fishtrap was in operation. An old Aleut, who had been a commercial sea otter hunter for a few years prior to 1911, offered an interesting measure of social change, the number of people who could survive if the supply ship did not come. He thought that perhaps six men knew enough ways of killing seals, catching fish, and collecting edible plants and shellfish, together with knowing how to build houses and make clothing to survive without outside intervention. Perhaps three men remain who could survive without external intervention. This criterion is a useful measure of social change. He was well aware that the cessation of sea otter hunting, the influenza epidemic, the collapse of fox trapping, the wreck of the *Umnak Native*, evacuation during the war, and the multitude of other changes had greatly affected Aleut life. But he recognized the more important fact that Aleuts could change their economy and still be Aleuts, although not real Aleuts in the sense of self-sufficiency.

INFLUENCE OF EXTERNAL EVENTS

Cataloging historical events provides some help in understanding the dissolution of this culture and of its resolution, but evaluating the events for both internal and external effects is difficult and may be subjective (Berreman, 1953). The increasing influence of external events is most obvious.

An experienced pioneer Alaskan pilot, Bob Reeve, established the first regularly scheduled airline in the Aleutians. Although weather conditions in the air are little better than those on the sea, he assembled what may well be the world's best pilots

Fig. 52. Fishing boats and processing ship at Dutch Harbor, Unalaska. The Aleut Corporation is actively moving into such commercial endeavors.

to captain the Reeve Aleutian Airways planes. They developed the capability to maintain passenger, mail, and freight service to many villages in the Aleutians and to St. Paul Island in the Pribilofs as well as to military bases. Aside from incredible emergency flights, also flown by Coast Guard and Navy planes from Adak or Kodiak depending upon the situation, the regularity of air delivery has brought many changes. With the lifting of restrictions on visiting the Pribilof Islands and freedom for Pribilof Aleuts to visit outside, the Aleutian and Pribilof Aleuts can intervisit much more easily. Several Aleuts have been employed by Reeve for many years. There is a genuinely personal touch between the plane crews and the villagers, especially with the stewardesses. An Aleut lady can quickly measure a stewardess for a handknit sweater, and the stewardesses can deliver flowering plants unbroken. The movement of freshly smoked silver salmon has been promoted as well as other choice foods, and these are especially appreciated on the Pribilofs where there are no salmon.

Aleut village communities are tough, durable, and very adaptable. Their independent attitude, their acephalic democracy, and the great degree of internalization of social behavior patterns enables them to be highly absorbent without losing their coherence. There has been a decline in quantity and use of natural resources, a loss of decision-making power within the village, and an increase in interagency ambiguity. The numbers of people have declined and their self-

Fig. 53. The village of Akutan looking across Akutan Bay. The remains of the abandoned whaling station are on the far side toward the right. Processing ships for king crab anchor in the bay and provide jobs in this growing industry.

sufficiency has diminished. Dependency on firearms, gasoline engines, dimension lumber, and on hospital services and an increase in the use of cash has diminished the fabricational and dietary self-sufficiency of early periods. The acknowledged need to be educated has taken on a new form. Therefore, the minimum number of children necessary to justify a school teacher is a new kind of problem that they discuss in detail. Dependence upon a hospital in Anchorage removes people from the village—children as well as adults—for varying periods, just as employment on fishing boats, in king crab canneries, or in fur seal processing on the Pribilofs take people out of the village community (Figs. 52 and 53). The mate shortage, intimately related to the numbers of school children, results in some outmigration, which, in turn, fuels the problem of mate shortage.

Nevertheless, the villages continue on. Predictions of their collapse have proven more fragile than the villages. The Attuans have accommodated to living with the Atka people, although they much prefer to return to their own village. Dialect identification is still a major factor in Aleut social life. Aleuts are proud to be Aleuts and they often return from great distances after long absences to resume residence. They do want to regain control over their land and their resources and participate in the larger American community with as many options as other American citizens. With their demonstrated skill in human adaptability, they may survive another 9000 years.

GLOSSARY

Acupuncture: Treatment of diseases by thrusting needles into body. Fixed points were traditionally used and places indicated by immediate disease variation. Regular blood letting was also practiced.

Alcidae: The family name for the alcids; puffins, murres. These are cliff-nesting birds; important for their eggs and for their skins, which were used for clothing. Puffins and murres were commonly eaten as well.

Aleut: The origin of the name is obscure (see Knud Bergsland). The Aleuts have their own language, race, and culture and were the exclusive inhabitants of the Aleutian ecosystem extending from Attu Island in the west to the Shumagin Islands and Port Moller in the east. Their own name for themselves is *unangan* (plural).

Algae: Any of a group of chiefly aquatic nonvascular plants, including seaweed, stonewarts, and pond scums. Ulva is one of the commonly eaten green algaes in the Aleutians.

Amak: A small island a few miles northwest of Cold Bay on the Alaska Peninsula. This is the older Aleut word for "walrus." In Russian the island is designated Walrus Island. Many walrus came here. Sea lion are more common there today.

Anangula: Ananiuliak Island on sailing charts. Anangula is a variant of the old Aleut name. A small island on the northwest side of Nikolski Bay, formerly part of Umnak Island. The oldest archeological site on the Bering Sea (8700–7200 years ago) is located on the southern end. It is a bird sanctuary for many species of birds: puffins, cormorants, eider ducks, whiskered auklets, eagles, and gulls.

Antiquities Act: An Act for the preservation of American Antiquities and accompanying uniform Rules and Regulations, approved June 8, 1906 (34 Stat. L., 225), it protects archeological sites on federally controlled lands. Permits must be secured from the Department of the Interior. Such sites must be excavated in approved fashion and the objects recovered must be catalogued, placed in museum or university collections, and be accessible to research and viewing. They cannot be bought or sold.

Baidarka: A small Aleut skin boat (Russian word; *kayak* in Eskimo). The word may be used for the one-hatch, two-hatched, or three-hatched kayak. The one- and two-hatch were in use before the Russians. The three-hatched form was invented by Aleuts to accommodate an administrator or cleric who rode in the middle hatch. The *baidarka* was decked over; the paddler wore a waterproof shirt secured to the hatch, making the boat watertight.

Barabora, barabara: Underground house (Siberian word). Framing structure of hewn timbers and planks of driftwood; roofed with timbers of whalebone, wood, matting, and sod. Originally had entry by a hole in the roof with descent ladder. After about 1800 a door was placed in the side. Walls above ground were sodded with the entry room called *kalador*. Some were very large and were occupied by several families.

Bidarshik: Commander or head of a trading post (Russian). It is derived from the Russian word *baidar*, or *bidar* (also *baidara*), applied to the large open skin boat of the Aleuts (*ighalogh*). The Eskimo word for the large open boat (*umiak*) is much better known outside the Aleutians.

Bone mineral content: The amount or mass of bone per unit area (gr/cm). Bone mineral content is measured by photon absorptiometry using a gamma source. The reading, which is direct and noninvasive, is comparable between living persons and their skeletal antecedents. Aleuts have high bone mineral, while Eskimos have low bone mineral.

Burin: Anangula burins are transverse burins made by striking a long flake transversely across the end of a snapped prismatic blade. Similar burins are found in Japan and Siberia, but not in Alaska. They may have been used for skin working, but not for cutting bone.

Camps: Aleut camps belong to particular members of a village and are inherited, bought, or sold. They may be many miles from the village and on another island. They may be used in winter or summer. They enhance the ability of a village group to exploit the resources of its area and they also provide a social and physical change of scenery for the families.

Chagak: *Chagak* is the Aleut word for "obsidian." (Cape Chagak, Umnak Island, designates the area where obsidian was mined for manufacture into tools such as scrapers, points, knives.)

Chaluka: The Aleut name of the large, 4000-year-old village site on the south side of the present village of Nikolski, Umnak Island. No definite meaning is known for the word. An unvoiced ending is omitted in the English rendition of the Aleut.

Chiefs: Under Russian administration a system of three chiefs—first, second, and third—administered village affairs. Under later revision, these have been converted to President, Vice-President, and Secretary-Treasurer.

Cores: Stones from which blades have been struck by a hammer blow (percussion flaking). A flat platform is formed by flake removal and then blades (symmetrical, prismatic flakes) are struck from the sides. The blades are used and the core is what remains. Core tablets are broad flakes removed from the top or "striking platform" when it becomes too battered.

Cortical thickness: The thickness of the cortical or dense bone in the shaft of a long bone. Cortical thickness can be measured by X ray in living persons or by the removal of a bone core in skeletons. Aleuts have thick cortical bone, while Eskimos have much thinner shafts of the long bones. Cortical thickness and bone mineral content are highly correlated.

Cossack: The Aleuts used this term for all Russians. Only a few Russians held the rank of Cossack, which had a military obligation. Cossacks also carried cord-bound books for keeping records, especially for the collection of *iasak* (*yasak*), a tribute or tax imposed on Aleut hunters.

Dual ending: A dual ending on an Aleut word indicates two or a pair of things. Thus the two hip bones, or one hip bone, can be indicated by the ending of the word.

Ecology: The interaction of whole organisms and groups of organisms with each other and with their environment.

Ecosystem: The total interactions of organisms, energy, matter, cycles, and climates. The Aleutian ecosystem utilizes energy from the sea, chemical nutrients, small organisms, larger organisms, invertebrates (fish, sea mammals, birds, and marine and land plants), and the Aleuts.

Harpoon: Harpoons generally have a detachable head that remains in the animal but is connected to the shaft by a line; lances and spears generally have fixed heads. Harpoon heads were made of whalebone or of ivory (sperm whale tooth or walrus). The styles vary geographically and with time.

Inheritance (Aleut):   There are many rules for inheritance of property, such as houses, campsites, books, and guns. The position of headman, or chief, was not inherited. Throwing boards passed from father or grandfather to son.

Kadagada: Image of the deity. A carved human figure, often suspended by the head from the ceiling inside the house. It is a representation of the paramount divinity, a "person" of the universe. He was concerned with hunting luck, protection from harm, and the reincarnation of souls.

Koniag (Konyag):   Koniags are Eskimos, not Aleuts. They inhabit Kodiak Island and a portion of the Alaska Peninsula from Cape Douglas to Kupreanof Point on the south side as well as some territory across the Peninsula. The Russians used the term *Aleut* for them, and much confusion exists in the census and early historical accounts as a consequence. Koniag Eskimo and Aleut are not mutually intelligible languages.

Labret: Lip decorations of ivory, bone, or stone. Carved and polished pieces with a flange are inserted into a hole, or holes (if there are two) in each corner of the lower lip from the inside. Later styles in use at the time of Russian discovery often resembled a bowler hat. Labret facets are often found on the lower teeth of skeletons.

Life expectancy: The average remaining years of life to be lived by a member of an age cohort, once having reached a given age. If, for example, life expectancy at age 10 is 45 years, then a person age 10 would, on the average, live an additional 45 years, or to age 55. Aleuts have long life expectancies in comparison to Eskimos and other native Americans.

Longevity: The actual length of life of an individual. Longevity is an individual measure, while life expectancy is a population or group measure. Many Aleuts enjoyed great longevity (greater than age 80). This is true for Aleuts before Russian contact as well as today. Age at death in skeletons can be determined accurately by photon–osteon analysis, which measures the bone mineral content and cortical thickness and determines the number and size of osteons by light microscopy.

Midden: Short form of kitchen midden, from Danish. Refers to the refuse or occupational debris of human occupation. The term has been used interchangeably with *mound* in the Aleutians where the village sites often take the form of stratified mounds.

Molar teeth: The large, flattened cheek teeth behind the incisors, canines, and premolars. The Aleuts have a high frequency of first lower molars with three roots, and a high frequency of absent third molars and reduced, or peg-shaped, third molars.

Mummies: Dead persons were prepared for mummification by sophisticated techniques, carefully wrapped in their clothing and matting, tied securely in a bundle, and placed in a cave, rock shelter, log tomb, or other sacred place. Many Aleut mummies have been preserved in the Smithsonian Institution.

Moxa: A wad of grass or other plant substance placed against the skin and fired, for medical treatment.

Ownership: Houses, harpoons, lamps, and so forth, all had individual owners. Ownership marks were often employed on harpoon heads. Hunting and collecting areas were under the control of the village or village constellation that dominated the area. Ownership rights are scrupulously observed by Aleuts.

Parka: An outer garment with hood and no opening in front (Siberian word usually pronounced "parki"). The Aleut waterproof shirt (*kamleika* in Russian) is a parka. In the Aleutians, the term *parka* was also used for the *sugh*, or *sux*. A garment made of birdskins, extending to the calves, with an upright collar, but no hood.

Prasnik: A holiday in the Russian Orthodox calendar. There are 86 holidays in addition to Sundays. The word is also used to indicate a party or celebration.

Promyshleniks: Fur hunters or trappers who, in practice, were explorers and conquerors. Originally, in Siberia, they worked for themselves. They were skilled land hunters but were unfamiliar with sea mammal hunting from *baidarkas*. Some used crossbows as well as traps and nets.

Pump (*muma*—Aleut form of Russian):   A wooden cigar-shaped tube, about the length of the forearm. Used for bailing out the *baidarka* and later used for bailing dories. The water is sucked up, the end of the tube is closed with an index finger and is emptied over the side.

Spalga: A Russian officer's sword with straight blade. Such a sword was taken from Jacob and used to cut his throat in the Massacre of the Denis Medvedev party at Chaluka in 1764. The Russian word lacks an Aleut ending.

Throwing board (*atlatl*):   Many harpoons and lances were thrown by this lever, one cubit in length (elbow to end of middle finger), with a hook to engage the butt of the harpoon at the far end, and a hole to engage the index finger at the handle end. It provided leverage for a faster and farther cast and was used with one hand. It was essential for a single man in a *baidarka*.

Toyon, tyown or *tyone*:   Term for chief or headman. Introduced by Russians.

Transition culture: The culture succeeding the Anangula unifacial burin, blade, and core culture, approximately 7200–4200 years ago. Burins are retained, with other blade tools, but bifacial tools flaked on both surfaces are added, some made on blades. Anangula village site yielded the type series in stratigraphic context.

Upwelling: Deep ocean water rises to the surface bringing nutrients up and promoting mixing of nutrients, oxygen, and solar radiation. An inertial (permanent) upwelling system in Samalga Pass enriches the upper waters to produce enormous faunal wealth of plankton for fish, birds, whales, and other sea mammals. Vertical mixing of water may also be aided by winds.

CITED AND RECOMMENDED READING

Alexander, Fred. "A Medical Survey of the Aleutian Islands." *New England Journal of Medicine*, 1949, *240*: 1035–1040.

Befu, Harumi. "Eskimo Systems of Relationship Terms—Their Diversity and Uniformity." *Arctic Anthropology*, 1964, *2*,(1): 84–98.

Bergsland, Knut. "Aleut Dialects of Atka and Attu." *Transactions of the American Philosophical Society*, 1959, *49*, Part 3.

Berreman, Gerald D. "Inquiry Into Community Integration in an Aleutian Village." *American Anthropologist*, 1955, *57*(1): 49–59.

Bisset, N. G. "Hunting Poisons of the North Pacific Region." *Lloydia*, 1976, *39* (2–3): 87–124.

Black, Lydia T. "Ivan Pank'kov—An Architect of Aleut Literacy." *Arctic Anthropology,* 1977, *XIV* (1): 94–107.

Byers, F. M. Jr. "Geology of Umnak and Bogoslof Islands, Aleutian Islands." *Geological Survey Bulletin* 1028-L. Washington, D.C.: U.S. Government Printing Office, 1959.

Chamisso, A. "Cetaceorum maris Kamtschatici imagines, ab Aleutis e ligno fictas, adumbravit recensuitque." *Verhandlungen der Kaiserlichen Leopoldnisch-Carolinischen Akademie der Naturforscher,* 1825, *4*(1): 249–262 (Nova Acta, *12*, pt. 1).

Chevigny, Hector. *Russian America: The Great Alaskan Venture 1741–1867.* New York: Viking, 1965.

Coxe, William. *Account of the Russian Discoveries Between Asia and America.* London: T. Cadell, 1780.

Dall, William H. *Alaska and Its Resources.* Boston: Lee and Shepard, 1870.

————. "On the Remains of Later Pre-historic Man Obtained from Caves in the Catherina Archipelago, Alaska Territory and Especially from Caves of the Aleutian Islands." *Smithsonian Contributions to Knowledge.* Washington, D.C.: Smithsonian Institution, 1878.

Elliott, Henry W. *Our Arctic Province.* New York: Scribner, 1887.

Fedorova, Svetlana G. *The Russian Population in Alaska and California, Late 18th Century–1867.* Translated and edited by Richard A. Pierce and Alton S. Donnelly. Kingston, Ontario: The Limestone Press, 1973.

Finney, Gertrude E. *To Survive We Must Be Clever.* New York: McKay, 1966.

Geoghegan, Richard H. *The Aleut Language.* Edited by Fredericka I. Martin. Washington, D.C.: U.S. Department of the Interior, 1944.

Golder, F. A. *Bering's Voyages.* New York: American Geographical Society Research Series, Nos. 1 and 2, 1922 and 1925.

Gsovski, Vladimir. *Russian Administration of Alaska and the Status of the Alaskan Natives.* Washington, D.C.: Prepared by the Chief of the Foreign Law Section, Law Library of the Library of Congress, U.S. Senate, Eighty-first Congress, Second Session, Document No. 152, 1950.

Hammerich, L. L. "The Origin of the Eskimo." *Proceedings of the Thirty-second International Congress of Americanists,* Copenhagen, Denmark, 1958, pp. 640–644.

Harper, Albert B. "Secular Change and Isolate Divergence in the Aleutian Population System." Ph.D. Thesis, University of Connecticut, Storrs, Conn., 1975. University Microfilm #BWH76-07188, Ann Arbor, Michigan 48106.

————. "Life Expectancy and Population Adaptation: The Aleut Centenarian Approach." In W. S. Laughlin and A. B. Harper, eds., *The First Americans: Origins, Affinities and Adaptations.* New York: Gustav Fischer, 1979, pp. 309–330.

————. "Origins and Divergence of Aleuts, Eskimos and American Indians." Unpublished manuscript, November 16, 1979.

Hopkins, David M. "The Cenozoic History of Beringia." In David M. Hopkins, ed., *The Bering Land Bridge.* Stanford, Cal.: Stanford University Press, 1967, pp. 451–484.

————. "Landscape and Climate of Beringia during Late Pleistocene and Holocene Time." In W. S. Laughlin and A. B. Harper, eds., *The First Americans.* New York: Gustav Fischer, 1979, pp. 15–41.

Hrdlička, Aleš. "Exploration of Mummy Caves in the Aleutian Islands." *Scientific Monthly,* 1941, *52*, Part I: 5–23; Part II: 113–130.

————. *The Aleutian and Commander Islands.* Philadelphia: Wistar Institute of Anatomy and Biology, 1945.

Hulten, Eric. *Flora of the Aleutian Islands,* 2d ed. London: Codicote, Herts, Wheldon & Wesley, Ltd., London and New York: Hafner, 1960.

Ivanov, S. V. "Aleut Hunting Headgear and Its Ornamentation." *Proceedings of the Twenty-third International Congress of Americanists,* 1930, pp. 477–504.

Jochelson, Waldemar. *Archaeological Investigations in the Aleutian Islands.* Washington, D.C.: Carnegie Institution, Publication No. 367, 1925.

———. *History, Ethnology and Anthropology of the Aleut.* Washington, D.C.: Carnegie Institution, Publication No. 432, 1933.

Krauss, Michael E. "Eskimo-Aleut." *Current Trends in Linguistics,* 1973, *10:* 796–902.

———. *Native Peoples and Languages of Alaska* (Map). Fairbanks: Alaska Native Language Center, 1974.

Laughlin, Sara B., William S. Laughlin, and Mary E. McDowell. "Anangula Blade Site Excavations, 1972 and 1973." Fairbanks, Alaska: *Anthropological Papers of the University of Alaska,* 1975, *17*(2): 39–48.

Laughlin, William S. "The Alaska Gateway Viewed from the Aleutian Islands." In W. S. Laughlin, ed., *Physical Anthropology of the American Indian.* New York: Viking, 1951, pp. 98–126.

———. "Decline of the Aleuts." Unpublished report to Governor Ernest Gruening, 1951.

———. "The Aleut-Eskimo Community." Fairbanks, Alaska: *Anthropological Papers of the University of Alaska,* 1952, *1*(1): 25–46.

———. "Eskimos and Aleuts: Their Origins and Evolution." *Science,* 1963, *142* (3593): 633–645.

———. "Human Migration and Permanent Occupation in the Bering Sea Area." In David M. Hopkins, ed., *The Bering Land Bridge.* Stanford, Cal.: Stanford University Press, 1967, pp. 409–450.

———. "Hunting: An Integrating Biobehavioral System and Its Evolutionary Importance." In R. B. Lee and I. Devore, eds., *Man the Hunter.* Chicago: Aldine, 1968.

———. "Ecology and Population Structure in the Arctic." In G. A. Harrison and Anthony J. Boyce, eds., *Demography and the Biological and Social Structure of Human Populations.* Oxford, Eng.: Clarendon Press, pp. 379–392.

———. "Aleuts: Ecosystem, Holocene History and Siberian Origin (Soviet and U.S. Scientists Join in a Study of the Origins of the First Americans)." *Science,* 1975, *189*(4202): 507–515.

Laughlin, William S., and Albert B. Harper, eds. *The First Americans: Origins, Affinities and Adaptations.* New York: Gustav Fischer, 1979.

Laughlin, William S., J. B. Jørgensen, and B. Frøhlich. "Aleuts and Eskimos: Survivors of the Bering Land Bridge Coast." In W. S. Laughlin and A. B. Harper, eds., *The First Americans: Origins, Affinities and Adaptations.* New York: Gustav Fischer, 1979, pp. 91–104.

Laughlin, William S., and Gordon H. Marsh. "A New View of the History of the Aleutians." *Arctic,* 1951, *4*(2): 75–88.

———. "The Lamellar Flake Manufacturing Site on Anangula Island in the Aleutians." *American Antiquity,* 1954, *20*(1): 27–39.

Laughlin, William S., and W. G. Reeder, eds. "Studies in Aleutian-Kodiak Prehistory, Ecology and Anthropology." *Arctic Anthropology,* 1966, *III*(2).

Lyapunova, Rosa G. *Essays in Aleut Ethnography.* In Russian. Leningrad: Science Publishers, 1975.

Makarova, R. V. *Russians on the Pacific: 1743–1799.* Kingston, Ontario: Limestone Press, 1975.

Marsh, Gordon H. "A Comparative Survey of Eskimo-Aleut Religion." Fairbanks, Alaska: *Anthropological Papers of the University of Alaska,* 1954, *3*(1): 21–36.

Marsh, Gordon H., and William S. Laughlin. "Human Anatomical Knowledge Among the Aleutian Islanders." *Southwestern Journal of Anthropology,* 1956, *12*(1): 38–78.

Marsh, Gordon H., and Morris Swadesh. "Kleinschmidt Centennial V: Eskimo Aleut Correspondences." *International Journal of American Linguistics*, 1951, *17* (4).

Milman, Ephy. "Dichotic Listening and Handedness: Preliminary Findings on the Aleut Population." Storrs, Conn.: University of Connecticut Report Series No. 12, Laboratory of Biological Anthropology, Biobehavioral Sciences Department, 1973.

Moorrees, Coenraad F. A. *The Aleut Dentition*. Cambridge, Mass.: Harvard University Press, 1957.

Murie, Olavs J. "Fauna of the Aleutian Islands and Alaska Peninsula, with Notes on Invertebrates and Fishes Collected in the Aleutians, 1936–38 by Victor B. Scheffer." Washington, D.C.: U.S. Government Printing Office, Handbook Number 61, *North American Fauna*, 1959.

Okladnikov, A. P., and R. S. Vasilievsky. *On Alaska and the Aleutian Islands*. Novosibirsk, U.S.S.R.: "Science" Publishing House, 1976.

Okun, S. G. *The Russian-American Company*. Cambridge, Mass.: Harvard University Press, 1951.

Porcher, C. Gadsen. "Basketry of the Aleutian Islands." *The Basket (The Organ of the Basket Fraternity)*, 1904, *2* (2): 67–79.

Ransom, J. Ellis. "Writing As a Medium of Acculturation Among the Aleut." *Southwestern Journal of Anthropology*, 1945, *1* (3): 333–344.

Salamatov, Lavrenty. "Travel Journal of Priest Lavrenty Salamatov, Atka (1862–1863)." *Alaska History Research Project: 1936–1938*. Unpublished report, Division of Documents, Library of Congress, Washington, D.C.

Spaulding, A. C. "Archaeological Investigations on Agattu, Aleutian Islands." Ann Arbor, Mich.: *Anthropological Papers*. Museum of Anthropology, The University of Michigan, No. 18, 1962.

Stejneger, Leonhard Hess. *The Russian Fur-Seal Islands*. U.S. Fish Commission Bulletin, Vol. 16. Washington, D.C.: U.S. Government Printing Office, 1896.

———. *Georg Wilhelm Steller: The Pioneer of Alaskan Natural History*. Cambridge, Mass.: Harvard University Press, 1936.

Stewart, T. Dale. *The People of America*. New York: Scribner, 1973.

Turner, Christy G., II. "Three-rooted Mandibular First Permanent Molars and the Question of American Indian Origins." *American Journal of Physical Anthropology*, 1971, *34* (2): 229–242.

———. "The Aleuts of Akun Island." *The Alaska Journal*, 1976, *16* (1): 25–31.

Turner, L. M. *Contributions to the Natural History of Alaska*. Washington, D.C.: U.S. Government Printing Office, U.S.A. Signal Service, Arctic Series No. 11.

Veniaminov, Innocent. *Notes on the Islands of the Unalaska Division*, 2 vols. In Russian. St. Petersburg: Greater Russian-American Co., 1840.

———. *An Essay upon the grammar of the Fox dialect of the Aleutian language*. In Russian. St. Petersburg: Imperial Academy of Sciences, 1846.

Waxell, Sven. *The American Expedition. With an Introduction and Note by M. A. Michael*. London: William Hodge and Company, Ltd., 1952.

Weyer, Edward Moffat, Jr. "An Aleutian Burial." *Anthropological Papers of the American Museum of Natural History*, 1929, *XXXI*: 219–238.

———. "Archaelogical Material from the Village Site at Hot Springs, Port Moller, Alaska." *Anthropological Papers of the American Museum of Natural History*, 1930, *XXXI*, Part IV: 239–279.

Zimmerman, Michael R., G. W. Yeatman, H. Sprinz, and W. P. Titterington. "Examination of an Aleutian Mummy." *Bulletin of the New York Academy of Medicine*, 1971, *47*: 80–103.